A BRIEF HISTORY

OF THE

MODERN AMERICAN

CONSERVATIVE

MOVEMENT

The
Heritage Foundation

A BRIEF HISTORY
OF THE
MODERN AMERICAN
CONSERVATIVE
MOVEMENT

by Lee Edwards

CONTENTS

PREFACE

Writing in 1950, in the introduction to *The Liberal Imagination*, literary critic Lionel Trilling announced that "liberalism is not only the dominant but even the sole intellectual tradition" in the United States. What he called the conservative impulse was not thoughtful at all, he averred, but was made up of at best "irritable mental gestures which seem to resemble ideas."

When Russell Kirk wrote *The Conservative Mind* in 1953—looking to posit Edmund Burke and Alexis de Tocqueville, as well as John Adams, Alexander Hamilton, and John Marshall, as conservative thinkers—Arthur Schlesinger, Jr., asserted in his book review that this "great scurrying about" for respectability produced only "an odd and often contradictory collection of figures" that did not rise "to the dignity of a conservative tradition."

In *The Liberal Tradition in America*, Louis Hartz explained that by conservatism, what was really meant was European feudalism, which was not only absent from, but altogether foreign to the American experience. He reiterated the then-established view that liberalism—meaning that which leads to modern American political liberalism, culminating in the New Deal and anticipating the Great Society—was the *only* tradition in the United States. In *Conservatism in America*, Clinton Rossiter concluded that because America was "a progressive country with a liberal tradition," conservatism in the United States was, simply put, "irrelevant."

When the existence of conservative thinkers and conservative political rumblings had to be explained, the intellectuals turned to derision. Richard Hofstadter, the Pulitzer Prize-winning historian, portrayed conservatism as a "paranoid style," nothing more than "symbolic politics," and the product of "status anxiety"—an aberration from the academic conventions of the day. "When, in all our history," he once wrote scornfully of Barry Goldwater, "has anyone with ideas so bizarre, so archaic, so self-confounding, so remote from the basic American consensus, ever got so far?" So much for objective scholarship.

That the leading minds of the American academy have always misunderstood conservatism, the conservative movement in American politics, and the relationship of conservative thought to the American political tradition goes without saying. The leading lights at our best universities still don't understand. Only recently, a team of learned professors from the University of California at Berkeley, Stanford University, and the University of Maryland argued in a leading psychology journal that conservatism is a pathology stemming from fear, aggression, uncertainty avoidance, irrational nostalgia, and the need for "cognitive closure."

It is no surprise that such elite thinkers have never really grasped the challenge to their ideas made by conservatism in favor of an older liberalism, one that takes its bearings from a deeper tradition, looking to the American Founders, and, through Adam Smith, Edmund Burke and John Locke, back to the foundations of classical thought and biblical revelation at the heart of Western civilization.

Oh, how times have changed. Some 50 years later, these "irritable mental gestures" are widely recognized as a legitimate and robust collection of ideas, enunciated by top columnists and defended by leading scholars, embodied in powerful think tanks and influential foundations, and personified by political figures at every level of government, up to and including the American presidency. The rise and continuing influence of conservative ideas and arguments has been one of the most remarkable developments in modern American political history.

But let's not get ahead of ourselves, for therein lies the tale.

This publication is the first in a series of occasional booklets to be published by The Heritage Foundation, under the auspices of the B. Kenneth Simon Center for American Studies, on the "First Principles" of the American tradition of ordered liberty that we seek to conserve "for ourselves and our posterity," as it says in our Constitution. Future publications will cover a range of themes and topics, each aimed at explaining our most primary ideas—which often have been forgotten or rejected—and considering what those principles should mean for America today.

This series is motivated by a powerful observation: Those that lead our nation today—and those who will lead it tomorrow—must *know* and *understand* our first principles if they mean to vindicate those principles and see to it that they once again guide our country.

We choose to begin this series by reviewing the immediate context of the post–World War II revival of conservative thought in American politics, a revival that continues to thrive and to shape our political life. "The conservative movement in 20th century America held fast through hard and difficult years to its vision of truth," Ronald Reagan observed soon after becoming president. "And history must also say that our victory, when it was achieved, was not so much a victory of politics as it was a victory of ideas, not so much a victory for any one man or party as it was a victory for a set of principles."

We can think of no one better to write on this topic than Heritage's own Lee Edwards. In 1963, he was information director for the Draft Goldwater Committee; and in 1964, he was director of information for the Goldwater for President Committee during the nomination campaign and then served in the presidential campaign as deputy director of public relations. In 1967, he wrote one of the first political biographies of Ronald Reagan. Having been a participant of the conservative movement from its very beginning, Dr. Edwards has been its chronicler ever since.

This booklet, it should be noted, is intended to provide a brief, introductory history of the modern American conservative movement. Of course, there is much more to be said and to be read. To assist in that endeavor, Dr. Edwards has included an annotated bibliography of some essential books about modern American conservatism, which he has divided into fundamental books, recommended books, a few histories about the movement, and several books that shaped him personally.

As we open this conversation about "First Principles," The Heritage Foundation takes pleasure—and I take great personal pleasure—in beginning the series with this essay, by this author.

Matthew Spalding
Director, B. Kenneth Simon Center for American Studies
First Principles Series Editor

Chapter I

Conservative Minds

American politics has often been driven by political movements—
the abolitionists in the pre–Civil War period, the progressives
in the first third of the twentieth century, the champions of civil
rights in the 1950s and 1960s—which were inspired by ideas: an end
to slavery, a significant role for government in the economic and social
affairs of the nation, the elimination of discrimination in schools,
housing, voting, public accommodations, and other areas of American life. In the latter part of the twentieth century there emerged
another influential political movement—the conservative movement,
committed to the ideas of limited government, free enterprise, individual freedom, and traditional American values.

In the beginning American conservatism was diffuse, rudimenta-
ry, and often discordant. The danger of an ever-expanding state was
clear and seemed ever more likely, but American conservatives, a nat-
urally disputatious lot, could not agree on an appropriate response and
whether the greater danger lay at home or abroad. Then, in the spring
of 1945, a little book was published that served as the first great cat-
alyst of the American conservative movement.

It was a time when Eastern Europe and most of the Balkans had
been ceded to communism because of the Yalta agreements, when
the future course of Western Europe seemed likely to be determined

by socialist if not communist ideas, when Mao Zedong and his "agrarian reformers" were preparing to launch a civil war that would secure their control of China, and when political observers assumed that President Harry Truman would carry forward Franklin D. Roosevelt's New Deal, including an economic "bill of rights" for all citizens. The whole world looked to be turning Left. The American historian Mortimer Smith asserted that the "central fact" of the last 75 years had been the march to collectivism, and that one theme had dominated the proposals of the postwar planners: "The individual must surrender more and more of his rights to the state which will in return guarantee him what is euphemistically called security."[1]

In this hour of overweening statism, *The Road to Serfdom* helped lay the foundation for an intellectual and political counterrevolution. The author, Friedrich A. Hayek, a 45-year-old Austrian economist teaching at the London School of Economics, argued that government "planning leads to dictatorship" and the direction of economic activity inevitably means the "suppression of freedom."[2] Deeply disturbed by the collectivist signs all around him, Hayek proposed a different road—the road of individualism and classical liberalism. And he listed the personal virtues necessary to travel that road: independence and self-reliance, individual initiative and local responsibility, and "a healthy suspicion of power and authority."[3] Hayek emphasized he was not advocating a "dogmatic *laissez faire* attitude." Like the classical political economist Adam Smith, Hayek accepted a governmental role, carefully limited by law, that encouraged competition and the functioning of a free society.[4]

The first edition of *The Road to Serfdom* had been published in England the previous year and had gone through an impressive six printings. Winston Churchill read it before he gave his 1945 election radio address denouncing socialism as a threat to British liberties.[5] The New York publishers Macmillan and Harper, however, both rejected the book; a Harper editor claimed it was "overwritten" and left the reader "without any clue as to what line to take on thought or policy."[6] The University of Chicago Press was pleased to publish a U.S. edition in early 1945 that immediately sold well and was favorably received. In the lead review of the *The New York Times Book Review*, the libertarian journalist Henry Hazlitt termed *The Road to Serfdom* "one of the most important books of our generation," comparable in "power and rigor of reasoning" to John Stuart Mill's classic, *On Liberty*.[7] The book reached a mass American audience in April 1945 when *Reader's Digest*, which had a circulation of nearly nine million, published a condensed edition of *The Road to Serfdom* and placed it at the front of the magazine—the first time a book had ever been so featured. The Book-of-the-Month Club subsequently distributed one million copies of the *Digest* version—making *The Road to Serfdom* one of the most talked about conservative books of the post–World War II era.

Hayek was en route to America for a series of academic lectures when the *Reader's Digest* issue highlighting *Serfdom* appeared. By the time his ship arrived, the scholar had been transformed into a celebrity. His sponsors quickly organized a national speaking tour starting with Town Hall in New York City. "There were 3,000 people in the hall," Hayek remembered, "a veritable sea of expectant faces."[8] A hostile *New Republic* attributed Hayek's success to the promotional efforts of "chambers of commerce, advertising agencies, and big business." But H. Stuart Hughes, writing in *Commentary* a decade later, got it right when he wrote that the publication of *The Road to Serfdom* "was a major event in the intellectual history of the United States."[9] Hayek's "little book" was the first defining philosophical work of the modern conservative movement.

The Road to Serfdom's nationwide impact was made possible through the conjunction of a philosopher, F. A. Hayek; a popularizer, *Reader's*

Friedrich A. Hayek

(Born May 8, 1899; died March 23, 1992)

F. A. Hayek was one of the twentieth century's most influential writers and intellectuals, always committed to strengthening the foundations of a free society. A graduate of the University of Vienna, he received numerous awards and honors for his work including the Nobel Prize in Economic Sciences in 1974 and the Presidential Medal of Freedom in 1992.

CAREER

Officer, Austro–Hungarian Army (Italian Front), 1917–1918

Legal Consultant, Austrian Government, carrying out provisions of Peace Treaty, 1921–1926

Director, Austrian Institute for Economic Research (co-founded with Ludwig von Mises), 1927–1931

Tooke Professor of Economic Science and Statistics, University of London, 1931–1950

Founder, The Mont Pelerin Society, 1947; President, 1947–1960

Professor of Social and Moral Sciences, University of Chicago, 1950–1962

Professor of Economic Policy, University of Freiburg, 1962–1968

Professor of Economics, University of Salzburg, 1968–1977

SELECTED WRITINGS

Monetary Theory and the Trade Cycle, 1929

The Road to Serfdom, 1944

The Constitution of Liberty, 1960

Law, Legislation and Liberty (3 vols), 1973, 1975, 1979

The Fatal Conceit, 1988

RECOMMENDED BIOGRAPHY

Friedrich Hayek: A Biography, Alan Ebenstein, St. Martin's Press, 2001

NOTABLE QUOTE

"Economic control is not merely control of a sector of human life which can be separated from the rest; it is the control of the means for all our ends."

—*The Road to Serfdom*

THE DIFFERENCE HE MADE

"Hayek was the greatest philosopher of liberty during the twentieth century."
  —Biographer Alan Ebenstein, *Friedrich Hayek: A Biography*
"Morally and philosophically I find myself in agreement with virtually the whole of [*The Road to Serfdom*]; and not only in agreement with it, but in deeply moved agreement."
  —Economist John Maynard Keynes, quoted in *The Road to Serfdom*
"On the biggest issue of all, the vitality of capitalism, he was vindicated to such an extent that it is hardly an exaggeration to refer to the twentieth century as the Hayek century."
  —Author John Cassidy, *The New Yorker*, February 7, 2000

Digest; and a philanthropist, DeWitt Wallace. Wallace, the *Digest's* co-founder and editor in chief, personally ordered *Serfdom's* condensation in his magazine and prepared the way for the Book-of-the-Month Club's mass distribution. Among the many Americans who read the condensed version were two World War II veterans in their mid-30s—Ronald Reagan, a film actor eager to resume his career but soon to be plunged into Hollywood politics, and Barry Goldwater, a restless Phoenix, Arizona, businessman looking for a new challenge, perhaps in local politics. Both Reagan, a liberal Democrat, and Goldwater, a conservative Republican, responded enthusiastically to Hayek's emphasis on self-reliance and the indispensability of the individual, and his powerfully reasoned rejection of economic planning. Both acknowledged later the book's lasting influence on their lives.

Over the next 50 years, the same combination of conservative philosopher, popularizer, philanthropist, and politician occurred again and again. The philosopher would present his ideas, usually in an academic forum, which would be translated into the common idiom and disseminated by popularizers—journalists and the like. The attention of politicians would be caught and their imagination fired to introduce public policies and political platforms based on conservative ideas. All the while prescient philanthropists would underwrite the thinking of the philosophers, the journals of the popularizers, and the campaigns of the politicians. The history of American politics suggests that a political movement must have these continuing waves of ideas, interpretation, and action along with sufficient financial resources to be successful.

HAD ENOUGH?

The political debate over the future direction of the nation in the post–World War II era began in earnest in January 1946 with Truman's first State of the Union address, in which the Democratic president asked for another year of wage and price controls, along with the nationalization of the housing industry and federal control of all unemployment compensation. One Republican in particular was fed up with Democratic proposals to expand the role of government—Ohio's brilliant, blunt senior senator, Robert A. Taft. Taft had become the most powerful Republican in the Senate through his formidable intellect, his huge appetite for hard work and long hours, and his political integrity—his support could not be purchased by government contracts or swayed by personal relationships. Taft was the first member of a remarkable political quartet that would dominate conservative and Republican politics for the next five decades.

Taft described himself as a "liberal conservative." By liberal, he meant someone "who is willing to accept change, who believes in freedom for others, and is sufficiently open-minded to be able to consider any proposal that is made to him." By conservative, he meant someone "who knows and appreciates the importance of stability. While I am willing and ready to consider changes, I want to be darned sure—darned sure—that they are really better than what

6

we have."[10] His guiding legislative principle was whether a policy "increases or decreases the liberty of our people."[11]

Taft was also firmly anti-communist and anti-Soviet out of principle and because it was good politics. In the mid-term elections of November 1946, Republicans adopted the slogan, "Had Enough? Vote Republican!" An eager Taft campaigned across the East and the Midwest, charging that the Democrats "at Tehran, at Yalta, at Potsdam, and at Moscow pursued a policy of appeasing Russia, a policy which has sacrificed throughout Eastern Europe and Asia the freedom of many nations and millions of people."[12]

In addition to the debatable foreign policy of the Truman administration, most Americans had had enough of strikes (in 1946, there were some 5,000 work stoppages), high prices, and "government by crony." As one observer put it, Harry Truman woke up the morning after election night with "a bad cold and a Republican Congress"— the first since 1928.[13] The conservative press was ecstatic. *The Chicago Tribune* editorialized that Republicans had "won the greatest victory for the Republic since Appomattox."[14]

Such triumphalism was not shared by the small group of American and European intellectuals who gathered in April 1947 in the Hotel du Parc in Mont Pelerin sur Vevey, Switzerland, to discuss the possibility of a "liberal" (i.e., classical liberal or libertarian) revival and the formation of an association of individuals committed to the principles of a free society. The principal organizer and first president was Friedrich Hayek. The majority of the attendees were economists (including future Nobel laureates Milton Friedman and George Stigler) along with representatives of other academic disciplines and three journalists. The travel expenses and accommodations of the 22 Europeans in attendance were paid by Swiss sources, those of the 17 Americans by the William Volker Charities Trust of Kansas City.

Notwithstanding the Republican victory in the United States, the classical liberals assembled in Mont Pelerin were convinced that the "central values of civilization" were in danger. The place of the individual and the "voluntary group" had been undermined by "extensions of arbitrary power." Freedom of thought and expression were threatened by power-seeking minorities. These dire developments had been fostered by a historical view that denied "all absolute moral standards," questioned the rule of law, and contributed to a decline of belief in "private property and the competitive market."[15]

At the suggestion of Leonard Read (who had started the Foundation for Economic Education in America the preceding year), the assembled intellectuals adopted the Mont Pelerin Society as their name and declared their intention, through the exchange of ideas, to "contribute to the preservation and improvements of the free society."[16] The organization, said Milton Friedman, served as a "rallying point" for advocates of freedom who were badly outnumbered almost everywhere they looked.[17] The creation of the Mont Pelerin Society underscored the critical role that individuals play in the making of history—in this instance an "action intellectual," Hayek, and a sympathetic philanthropist, Harold Luhnow of the Volker Trust.[18]

The Mont Pelerin Society over the years became an international "who's who" of classical liberal and neo-liberal intellectuals, with attendance at its annual meetings now often exceeding 750 (20 times the number of those who attended the founding conference). But the founding of the Mont Pelerin Society in 1947 received scant notice in the establishment press in America and was ignored by modern liberals secure in their domination of the nation's ideas and politics.

THE CONSEQUENCE OF IDEAS

While Hayek and his libertarian colleagues were founding an organization, an unknown English professor at the University of Chicago was pondering the "fallacies of modern life" and whether and how it might be possible to preserve Western civilization. Richard M. Weaver was a Southerner, born in North Carolina and educated at the University of Kentucky and Vanderbilt University, where he was strongly influenced by the Agrarians, particularly John Crowe Ransom. After receiving his doctorate from Louisiana State University, Weaver joined the Chicago faculty in 1943 and taught there until his death in 1963. By late 1947, he had completed a book he wanted to call *The Fearful Descent*, but his publisher selected another title and in early 1948, *Ideas Have Consequences* appeared. Author Frank Meyer, who sought throughout his professional life to rationalize the different strains of conservatism, stated that Weaver's book was "the *fons et origo* [source and origin] of the contemporary American conservative movement."[19]

Richard Weaver argued that ideas like nominalism, rationalism, and materialism had led inexorably to what he saw as the moral "dissolution" of the West. Man had turned away from first principles and true knowledge and eagerly embraced rampant egalitarianism and the cult of the mass. But, conservative historian George Nash points out, Weaver was not content to write a jeremiad but offered three reforms—three ideas—that would help mankind recover from the scourge of modernism: a defense of private property, a purification and respect for language, and an attitude of piety toward nature, each other, and especially the past.[20]

The response to *Ideas Have Consequences*—the second defining philosophical work of modern American conservatism—was hot and cold. Liberal theologian Paul Tillich, liberal historian Reinhold Niebuhr, and educator John Crowe Ransom praised it highly. The philosopher Eliseo Vivas, then transitioning from liberalism to conservatism, called Weaver "an inspired moralist."[21] A considerably less sympathetic reviewer called the Southern Protestant author "a propagandist for a return to the medieval papacy." Another critic denounced the book as part of a University of Chicago Press "chain of reaction" that included books by political scientist Hans Morganthau (the father of *realpolitik*) and Friedrich Hayek.[22]

The latter critic was on to something. For all their philosophical differences, both Hayek and Weaver traced the decline of the West to "pernicious" liberal ideas. For Hayek, it was economic planning; for Weaver, moral relativism. Hayek proposed the alternative road of individual freedom within a framework of carefully limited government. Weaver insisted that a good society required a foundation of certain eternal truths. The two writers—and their works—represented the libertarian and the traditionalist strains of American conservatism that began to merge, if fitfully, under the twin threats of welfarism at home and communism abroad.

AN EXTRAORDINARY CONGRESS

Meanwhile, Senator Taft and his Republican colleagues in the House were striving hard to pass a conservative agenda in the 80th Congress. By the end of the first session, Republicans had succeeded in reducing Truman's budget by about 7.5 percent, and were pushing hard for a tax cut. Federal, state, and local taxes, Taft pointed out, represented 30 percent of the national income. Tax reduction, he insisted, was "essential to the welfare of the country, because the present heavy burden of taxation is an evil in itself."[23] But, when the Congress did pass tax reform in May 1947—cutting personal income taxes by 30 percent at lower income levels and 10.5 percent at the top—Truman quickly vetoed the bill. The measure, the president explained with impeccable liberal logic, would encourage consumer spending, stimulate inflation, and deprive the government of money that should be used to reduce the national debt. Truman also emphasized that the Republican bill favored the wealthy over the middle class and lower-income citizens—a classic Democratic argument that pitted class against class.

Although House Republicans overrode the president's veto, the Senate fell five votes short of the necessary two-thirds. Taft consoled himself with the expectation that the American people would force Democrats to approve a tax cut in the election year of 1948, which is what happened. The Taft plan of reduced government spending and tax cuts—a 1940s version of 1980s supply-side economics— was politically prudent and turned out to be econoically efficacious as well. Congress's 1948 tax cut proved to be non-inflationary.

Republicans believed they had taken a giant step toward recapturing the White House after 16 years of occupancy by Franklin D. Roosevelt and his unelected successor, Harry Truman. But they were puzzled by the lack of public enthusiasm for their program. They had reduced spending more than any other Congress in recent history. They had passed the historic Taft–Hartley Act reforming labor–management relations in response to the expressed wishes of most Americans. Yet, as *Human Events*, a weekly newsletter and the leading conservative publication of the day, pointed out, "There has been little evidence of public gratitude."[24] Robert Taft, the leader most closely associated with Congress's performance, saw his popularity as a potential presidential contender wane steadily as the session went on.

There were several reasons for the paradox. The establishment media—led by *The New York Times*—were not enthusiastic about the Republican proposals, particularly the tax cuts. No grassroots organizations were flooding congressional offices with telegrams, phone calls, and letters. And congressional leaders, from Taft to House Speaker Joseph Martin of Massachusetts, did not take the time to explain to the people what they were trying to do or to attempt to enlist their help. Then as now, Republicans almost seemed to resent the need to communicate with constituents. "The truth," wrote *Human Events* editor Frank Hanighen of the disconnect between the Republican Congress and the public, "is that we have not an effective non-governmental process here at home to make the public attitude intelligible to its representatives, and vice versa."[25] In the late 1940s, *Human Events* and a nascent American Enterprise Association (renamed the American Enterprise Institute in 1962) were among the few non-governmental institutions in Washington, D.C., that were explicitly conservative.

Another paradox prevailed in the summer of 1948. Despite the lukewarm public approval of Republicans, one man's political fate seemed sealed—President Truman's. Every public opinion poll reported that if Truman ran for the presidency, he would be soundly defeated. The percentage of Americans who thought the president was doing a good job had declined to an abysmal 36 percent.

Overly confident Republicans were so convinced they would win in November that they generously left the flags and bunting from their national convention in place for the cash-strapped Democrats, who were meeting in the same Philadelphia hall a few weeks later. However, the GOP presidential candidate was not the conservative Ohio senator who had led the 80th Congress through two productive years in Washington, but rather the establishment's favorite, New York Governor Thomas E. Dewey, who had given FDR a surprisingly close race in 1944. Republicans tilted toward Dewey because of a widespread feeling that Taft could not match Dewey as a vote getter.

Taft's chances were also hindered by the absence of a conservative movement that would have compensated for the senator's lack of personal appeal with organizational muscle. Dewey offered a way for Republicans to play it safe in an election whose conclusion they thought was foregone. But they failed to reckon with Truman's iron will and searing rhetoric. For 33 days that fall, aboard a railroad Pullman car, the president and his campaign team engineered one of the biggest upsets in modern political history. Although historians have rightfully noted Truman's plain-spoken rhetoric, remarkable stamina, and serene conviction that he would win as major factors in his victory, they have downplayed the effect of the president's deliberate distortions of Dewey, Taft, former President Herbert Hoover, and the so-called do-nothing 80th Congress.

Truman charged that a vote for Dewey was "a vote for fascism," mocked Taft as "a mossback still living back in 1890," demonized Hoover, and described Republicans as "gluttons of privilege" and the captives of "big business and the special interests."[26] Taft urged Dewey to fight back. "The only way to handle Truman," he said, "was to hit [him] every time he opened his mouth." But Dewey talked to confident party operatives around the country, read the polls that had him in the lead, and kept to the high road. He told Taft that over the years he had found that when he got into controversies, he lost votes—an observation Taft thought "disgraceful" for a practicing politician.[27]

Truman's narrow victory was the most unexpected electoral triumph in modern political history—not one major pollster or political analyst predicted the outcome. The president received 24,105,587 votes (49.5 percent) to Dewey's 21,970,017 votes (45.1 percent). Governor Strom Thurmond of South Carolina (running as a segregationist Dixiecrat) and former Vice President Henry Wallace (a pro-communist Progressive) each garnered fewer than 1.2 million votes. In the Electoral College, the tally was Truman 303, Dewey 189, Thurmond 38, and Wallace 0.

Disappointed conservatives consoled themselves that the Republican Party had learned that it should not nominate a candidate who

Barry Goldwater

(Born January 1, 1909; died May 29, 1998)

Known as "Mr. Conservative," Senator Barry Goldwater of Arizona offered a defiantly conservative choice in his 1964 campaign for the presidency. He was roundly defeated but laid a foundation for the conservative movement's political successes in 1980 and beyond. An accomplished airman, flying over 180 different aircraft in his lifetime, Goldwater organized and was chief of staff of the Arizona Air National Guard and a Major General in the Air Force Reserve.

POLITICAL CAREER

Phoenix City Council, 1949–1952

United States Senator (Arizona), 1953–1964, 1969–1986

Chairman, Republican Senatorial Campaign Committee, 1960

Presidential nominee (Republican), 1964

Chairman, Senate Armed Services Committee, 1985–1986

SELECTED WRITINGS

The Conscience of a Conservative, 1960

With No Apologies: The Personal and Political Memoirs of United States Senator Barry M. Goldwater, 1979

Goldwater, with Jack Casserly, 1988

RECOMMENDED BIOGRAPHY

Goldwater: The Man Who Made a Revolution, Lee Edwards, Regnery Publishing, 1995

NOTABLE QUOTE

"I would remind you that extremism in the defense of liberty is no vice! And let me remind you also that moderation in the pursuit of justice is no virtue!"

—Acceptance of presidential nomination, Republican National Convention, July 1964

THE DIFFERENCE HE MADE

"Again and again in American history it has happened that the losers of the presidency contributed almost as much to the permanent tone and dialogue of politics as did the winners."

—Political historian Theodore H. White, *The Making of the President—1964*

14

"There is no doubt that Barry Goldwater's message was Ronald Reagan's message...Goldwater really forged American politics for the next thirty years."
　—Pollster–strategist Richard B. Wirthlin, quoted in *Goldwater: The Man Who Made a Revolution*

"You set the pattern...I have tried to do the same."
　—Ronald Reagan to Barry Goldwater, after winning the Republican nomination for governor of California, June 1966

failed to carry the campaign to the opposition or to take decisive stands on the issues. It was reasonable to assume that Bob Taft would be the GOP's presidential nominee in 1952. If not, warned *The Chicago Tribune* in a blunt editorial, "the millions of patriotic men and women who have looked to [the Republican Party] for leadership will have to look elsewhere."[28]

"IRRITABLE MENTAL GESTURES"

Meanwhile, in his first bid for public office, Arizona businessman Barry Goldwater was easily elected to the Phoenix City Council, leading a field of 27 candidates. Hollywood actor Ronald Reagan campaigned vigorously for fellow Democrat Harry Truman, whom he called "an outstanding president."[29] William F. Buckley, Jr., was elected chairman of the *Yale Daily News* and began writing about his school's alarming attitude about God and collectivism. Russell Kirk enrolled at the University of St. Andrews in Scotland and began working on his doctoral dissertation, which traced the prominent role of conservative thought in America since the Founding. As Matthew Spalding points out in the Preface, the liberal critic Lionel Trilling was scornful of any such thesis, stating that liberalism was not only the dominant but even the sole intellectual tradition in America. Although Trilling conceded that a conservative or reactionary "impulse" existed here and there, he insisted that conservatism expressed itself only in "irritable mental gestures which seem to resemble ideas."[30]

Hayek emphatically disagreed, declaring at a meeting of the Mont Pelerin Society that the period of intellectual drought regarding the ideas of freedom "seems to have come to an end." One proof was the appearance in the fall of 1950 of a new journal, *The Freeman,* which declared its dedication to "traditional liberalism and individual freedom."[31] Edited by the classical liberal journalists John Chamberlain and Henry Hazlitt, the fortnightly magazine featured such contributors as ex-FDR adviser Raymond Moley, columnist George Sokolsky, and author-broadcaster John T. Flynn. Not only professional journalists, but also scholars like Hayek, Ludwig von Mises, and German economist Wilhelm Roepke (who helped to guide Germany's "economic miracle" in the 1950s and 1960s), appeared in its pages. "It is difficult," wrote conservative historian George Nash, "to convey a sense of the crucial role of *The Freeman* at the height of its prestige between 1950 and 1954."[32]

At the time, the Left had a number of influential journals, including *The New Republic, The Nation, Commentary, The New Leader,* and *The Reporter.* The Right now had *The Freeman,* though that was not the only conservative alternative. Since 1944, the weekly *Human Events* had provided a platform for a wide variety of conservative writers and thinkers, including most of those who now appeared in *The Freeman.* However, unlike *Human Events,* which is still published 60 years after its birth, *The Freeman* was a financial disaster from the start and by mid-1954 had lost $400,000. It was purchased by Foundation for Economic Education President Leonard Read, who converted it into a monthly libertarian publication. Conservatives were disconsolate over the demise of *The Freeman* but would soon find consolation in the birth of the most important journal in the history of modern American conservatism, *National Review.*

But first came several other events that shaped the conservative movement—the conviction in 1950 of former Soviet spy Alger Hiss; the publication in 1951 of Bill Buckley's first book, *God and Man at Yale* (controversial and best-selling as most of his books would be); the appearance in 1952 of Whittaker Chambers's magisterial memoir, *Witness*, which would lead many into the conservative ranks (including *National Review* publisher William A. Rusher and acerbic newspaper columnist and television commentator Robert Novak); and the founding in 1952–1953 of conservatism's first youth organization, the Intercollegiate Society of Individualists, whose paradoxical name did not hinder it from attracting several thousand members on 200 college campuses in its first two years.

The Alger Hiss–Whittaker Chambers spy case of 1948–1950 was a defining event, with liberals passionately defending the Harvard-educated Hiss, whom they considered one of their own, and conservatives siding with *Time* editor Chambers and his congressional champion, Richard Nixon of California. Chambers reluctantly testified before the House Committee on Un-American Activities in 1948 that as an underground communist agent in the 1930s, he had known a young State Department official named Alger Hiss. Hiss vehemently denied the charge and sued for libel, forcing Chambers to produce secret government documents he had hidden in a pumpkin on his Maryland farm that proved the two men had been part of a Soviet espionage apparatus during the New Deal years. After two long, contentious trials, Hiss was convicted of perjury (the statute of limitations on espionage having lapsed) and was sentenced to four years in prison. The Right felt vindicated, the Left violated, perceiving that the generation of the New Deal had been as much on trial as Hiss himself. "The Hiss case," George Nash wrote, "forged the anti-Communist element in an emerging conservatism."[33]

God and Man at Yale was one of the most discussed books of 1951, listed as number 16 on *The New York Times* best-seller list one month after publication. Dedicating his work to God, country, and Yale, "in that order," Buckley charged that his alma mater had abandoned both Christianity and free enterprise, or what he called individualism. Buckley's chief "sin" in the eyes of his critics, wrote Yale alumnus John Chamberlain in his introduction, was that he held certain truths to be self-evident: "that the free economy is better for both the individual and the group than the 'planned' or the controlled economy; that man has a definite nature, which includes intimations of a moral and religious character; that to live 'solely' for others is not only an impracticability but an insult to the average human being's need and capacity for self-reliance."[34]

When Chambers published his 800-page autobiography, *Witness*, in 1952, it was an instant bestseller and for good reason: It was a dramatic story of spies, espionage, and betrayal and an apocalyptic warning about the epic battle being waged between the West and its totalitarian enemies. The book held special attraction for conservatives because it asserted (as conservatives had for years) that America faced a transcendent crisis, not a temporary one; that the crisis was one of faith, not simply politics or power; and that secular liberalism was as much an enemy as communism because it was at its roots another form of communism.[35]

Conservatives were also deeply worried about the American academy. By 1950, as the result of decades of missionary work by the Pragmatist philosopher John Dewey and his colleagues, most of the levers of American higher education were in the hands of an informal but cognizant coalition of pragmatists, progressives, and socialists. Parents were shocked at what their children were learning—and not learning—in colleges and universities. It was in this collectivist climate that the radical libertarian Frank Chodorov proposed (in *Human Events*) the creation of a network of campus clubs for individualist students. Chodorov wondered whether there was in America "a will for freedom of sufficient vigor to initiate the suggested campaign."[36]

Letters poured in, praising the proposed program, although some anxious parents argued that the educating should begin in kindergarten, not college. The names of several hundred individualistic students were collected, but no seed money was forthcoming. The idea simmered until Chodorov revisited the subject in a *Human Events* essay titled, "The Adam Smith Clubs." This time the responses included a $1,000 check from one of the most generous benefactors of the American conservative movement—Sun Oil Company founder J. Howard Pew.

With the encouragement of his editor-boss, Frank Hanighen, and after visiting Pew in his Philadelphia office, Frank Chodorov incorporated his idea in April 1952 under the name the Intercollegiate Society of Individualists. The articles of incorporation stated that the organization's objective was "to promote among college students, specifically, and the public, generally, an understanding of and appreciation for the Constitution of the United States of America, *laissez-faire* (free market) economics and the doctrine of individualism."[37] As with many other events that built the conservative movement in the last half of the twentieth century, the society's creation involved a philosopher (albeit of the homespun variety), Frank Chodorov; a popularizer, *Human Events*; and a philanthropist, J. Howard Pew.

1 Mortimer Smith, "Individualism Talks Back," *Christian Century* 62, February 14, 1945, p. 202, as quoted in George H. Nash, *The Conservative Intellectual Movement in America Since 1945* (Wilmington, Del.: Intercollegiate Studies Institute, 1996), p. 2.

2 Friedrich A. Hayek, *The Road to Serfdom, Reader's Digest* condensed version with Foreword by Edwin J. Feulner, Jr., and Introduction by John Blundell (London: *Readers' Digest,* 1999), p. 10.

3 *Ibid.*, p. 15.

4 *Ibid.*, pp. 6–7.

5 See Harold Macmillan, *Tides of Fortune* (New York: Harper Collins, 1969), p. 32.

6 R. M. Hartwell, *A History of the Mont Pelerin Society* (Indianapolis: Liberty Fund, 1995), p. 23.

7 Henry Hazlitt, "An Economist's View of 'Planning'," *New York Times Book Review,* September 24, 1944, p. 1.

8 Hayek, *The Road to Serfdom, Reader's Digest* condensed version, p. xv.

9 Friedrich A. Hayek, *The Road to Serfdom,* condensed version with foreword by Fred R. Glahe and introduction by Gerald P. O'Driscoll (Boulder, Colo., c. 1980), p. 3.

10 Caroline Thomas Harnsberger, *A Man of Courage: Robert A. Taft* (Chicago: Wilcox and Follett, 1952), p. 7.

11 Robert A. Taft, speech before the Young Republican Club of Lawrence County, Ohio, April 4, 1936, in Robert A. Taft Papers, Library of Congress; Russell Kirk and James McClellan, *The Political Principles of Robert A. Taft* (New York: Fleet Publishing, 1967), p. 62; James T. Patterson, *Mr. Republican: A Biography of Robert A. Taft* (Boston: Houghton Mifflin Company, 1972), p. 332.

12 Patterson, *Mr. Republican,* p. 313.

13 Joseph C. Goulden, *The Best Years: 1945–1950* (New York: Atheneum Publishers, 1976), pp. 231.

14 *Ibid.*, pp. 231–232.

15 Statement of Aims of the Mont Pelerin Society, as quoted in Hartwell, *History of the Mont Pelerin Society,* p. 41.

16 *Ibid.*, p. 52.

Conservative Minds

17 Nash, *The Conservative Intellectual Movement in America Since 1945*, p. 26.

18 Theodore White, "The Action Intellectuals," *Life*, June 15, 1967, p. 35.

19 Frank S. Meyer, "Richard M. Weaver: An Appreciation," *Modern Age*, (Summer–Fall 1970), p. 243.

20 Nash, *The Conservative Intellectual Movement in America Since 1945*, pp. 34–35.

21 *Ibid.*, p. 41.

22 W. E. Garrison, "Unraveling Mr. Weaver," *Christian Century*, May 5, 1948, p. 416, and George R. Geiger, "We Note … the Consequences of Some Ideas," *Antioch Review*, Vol. 8 (Spring 1948), p. 251.

23 Patterson, *Mr Republican*, p. 373.

24 Frank C. Hanighen, "Not Merely Gossip," *Human Events*, July 30, 1947, p. 5.

25 *Ibid.*

26 David McCullough, *Truman* (New York: Simon and Schuster, 1992), pp. 700, 661, 681, 658.

27 *Ibid.*, p. 696.

28 Irvin Ross, "What Happened in 1948," in Alonzo L. Hamby, ed., *Harry S. Truman and the Fair Deal* (Lexington: D.C. Heath and Company, 1974), p. 117.

29 Ronald Reagan, *An American Life* (New York: Simon and Schuster, 1990), p. 133.

30 Lionel Trilling, *The Liberal Imagination* (New York: Viking Press, 1950), p. ix.

31 Friedrich A. Hayek, "A Rebirth of Liberalism," *The Freeman*, July 28, 1952, p. 731, and "The Faith of the Freeman," *The Freeman*, October 2, 1950, p. 5.

32 Nash, *The Conservative Intellectual Movement in America Since 1945*, p. 17.

33 *Ibid.*, p. 100.

34 Introduction by John Chamberlain, in William F. Buckley, Jr., *God and Man at Yale* (Chicago: Regnery Publishing, Inc., 1951), pp. vii–viii.

35 *Ibid.*, pp. 91–93, and Whittaker Chambers, *Witness* (New York: Random House, 1952), pp. 741–742.

36 Frank Chodorov, "A Fifty-Year Project to Combat Socialism on the Campus," Intercollegiate Society of Individualists, 1952.

37 "Resume of Activities of Intercollegiate Society of Individualists, 1952–1953, 1953–1954," Intercollegiate Society of Individualists Files, Wilmington, Delaware.

Chapter 2

Movement Builders

WE LIKE IKE

Whatever liberal intellectuals like Lionel Trilling might say about the pervasiveness of liberalism, liberal politicians were finding it hard going. Eighteen months after the 1948 election, President Truman's popularity had slumped to the mid-30s as scandals involving several of his closest associates erupted. In the Senate, a bipartisan coalition led by Republican Robert Taft and Democrat Richard Russell prevented passage of most of the Fair Deal, which was not, in any event, generating much public enthusiasm. For conservatives, this was proof that Truman's victory had been a fluke. Conservatives argued that the Fair Deal was destined to fail because it was based on a political aberration: the New Deal. The New Deal had been adopted by Americans because they had lost confidence in themselves and their institutions during the Great Depression. They had reluctantly accepted what seemed to be the only realistic solution: a very large helping of big government.

Following FDR's death and the winning of World War II, Americans began reverting to a more traditional attitude toward government—less is better. Truman misread the 1948 results as an endorsement of liberalism when they were in fact a rejection of "me-too" Republicanism. Besides, only Roosevelt, the master politician, could have held together the disparate elements of the New Deal coalition, and Harry Truman was no FDR.

Although there were other candidates, like Harold Stassen, Earl Warren, and Douglas MacArthur, the 1952 Republican presidential nomination race was essentially between Dwight Eisenhower and Robert Taft, between the Eastern liberal wing and the Midwestern conservative wing of the GOP, between "modern" Republicans and "regular" Republicans, between pragmatists eager to win at almost any price and idealists as interested in principle as victory. In late June, half of the nation's top political reporters thought Taft would win the nomination, but in the polls, Ike led Taft 44 percent to 35 percent among Republicans and by an even larger margin among independent voters.

On the day before the Republican convention opened in Chicago, Taft held a news conference at which he displayed 530 telegrams from delegates pledged to him until hell froze over (604 votes would secure the nomination). There did not seem to be any way that the senator from Ohio could be denied what he had so clearly earned after 15 years of effective party leadership. But the Eisenhower forces found a way by challenging accredited delegates from the South who were strongly behind "Mr. Republican." Two Texas delegations showed up in Chicago, each claiming to be the legitimate representatives of the Lone Star State.

The convention officials were all Taft men, ready to approve the pro-Taft delegation, but the Eisenhower people denounced what they called "the Texas steal." Masked "bandits" roamed the Chicago streets carrying placards that read "Taft Steals Votes," while oversized signs hung from hotels proclaiming that "RAT" stood for "Robert A. Taft."[1] The convention delegates wanted to nominate Taft, but the polls showed Ike beating Governor Adlai Stevenson, the likely Democratic nominee, 59 percent to 31 percent, whereas

Taft and Stevenson were in a virtual tie. Republicans loved Taft, observed the historian William Manchester, but "they loved victory more."[2] When the Eisenhower Texas delegation was seated by a convention vote, control of the Republican Party passed to Eisenhower, who was nominated unanimously on the second ballot.

There were explanations aplenty as to why Taft lost the nomination (hubris, a mishandling of the Texas delegates question), but as important as any was the absence of a cohesive conservative movement, including people of financial means, that would have rallied to Taft's side. Those who should have been supporting Taft's limited government platform, Frank Hanighen wrote in *Human Events*, were "either stupidly donating money to foundations which oppose his ideas or complacently waiting for his triumph at the polls."[3]

The essential truth about Taft's failure to capture the 1952 nomination was that the Eastern states—the Eastern establishment—still ruled the Republican Party at convention time. The Eisenhower camp's dreams of victory, however, might have evaporated without the immediate public support of Taft, who, at a press conference with Ike, stated that he would do "everything possible in the campaign to secure his [Eisenhower's] election and to help in his administration."[4] Many conservative Republicans, however, were not so willing to forgive and forget how their hero had been denied what was rightfully his and resolved to take back the party one day.

The election results did not startle anyone, including the Democrats. Eisenhower captured 55.4 percent of the total popular vote and swept the Electoral College, 442 to 89. His coattails helped Republicans gain narrow majorities in both Houses of Congress. For the first time since 1932, Republicans controlled both the White House and Capitol Hill.

While the Republican triumph was due in large measure to General Eisenhower's extraordinary personal appeal (encapsulated in the campaign button, "I Like Ike"), other factors came into play. The Grand Old Party was a united party, thanks to Robert Taft. Many Catholic Democrats, especially those of Irish and Polish background, voted Republican because of the party's anti-communist rhetoric. *The New York Times'* Arthur Krock wrote that "the voting majority indicated approval of the objectives of what the Democrats and independents have assailed as McCarthyism."[5] Ike carried four Southern states because Taft and other conservatives forced him to the right. Also, Democratic candidate Adlai Stevenson was unable to hold together the old FDR coalition of big cities, organized labor, and minorities.

PROFILE IN COURAGE

In his inaugural address, Eisenhower repeated the tough, anti-communist themes of the campaign, declaring, "Freedom is pitted against slavery; lightness against dark." In his State of the Union address, he said that the United States would "never acquiesce in the enslavement of any people."[6] Ike was keeping faith with U.S. allies in Western Europe who faced a mighty Soviet phalanx held in check only by American might and will. And he was reassuring congressional conservatives who were watching the White House closely for any sign of foreign policy flinching.

While loyal to the president, Taft strictly controlled the Senate, effectively isolating the mandarins of the Eastern establishment. He also sought to contain an eager Joe McCarthy by denying him the chairmanship of what most observers assumed would be his province—the Internal Security Subcommittee of the Senate Judiciary Committee. Instead, Taft gave McCarthy the Government Operations Committee, an important post but normally not concerned with subversion and espionage. Meanwhile, Eisenhower actively courted his one-time rival and now essential team member,

Robert A. Taft

(Born September 8, 1889; died July 31, 1953)

Son of U.S. President William H. Taft, Senator Robert Taft of Ohio dominated the Senate and the Republican Party from the late 1930s to the early 1950s with his intellectual capacity, boundless energy, and political honesty, but never won his party's presidential nomination. He is best known legislatively for his authorship of the Taft–Hartley Act of 1947, which revised existing law to produce more equality in collective bargaining between labor and management.

POLITICAL CAREER

Ohio House of Representatives, 1921–1926

Speaker and Majority Leader, Ohio House of Representatives, 1926

Ohio Senate, 1931–1932

United States Senate (Republican), 1939–1953

Chairman, Committee on Labor and Public Welfare, 1939–1945

Presidential Candidate (Republican), 1940, 1948, 1952

Majority Leader, U.S. Senate, 1953

SELECTED WRITINGS

A Foreign Policy for Americans, 1951

RECOMMENDED BIOGRAPHY

Mr. Republican: A Biography of Robert A. Taft, James T. Patterson, Houghton Mifflin Company, 1972

NOTABLE QUOTE

"In seeking a guiding principle, I have come more and more to believe that the consideration which ought to determine almost every decision of policy today is the necessity of preserving, maintaining, and increasing the liberty of the people of our country."

—*Congressional Record,* February 25, 1953

THE DIFFERENCE HE MADE

"The Senate has lost one of its leading members of all time. The American people have lost a truly great citizen and I have lost a wise counselor and valued friend."

—President Dwight D. Eisenhower upon the death of Robert Taft, July 31, 1953.

"Taft spoke for constitution, self-government, private rights, the rule of law, security, peace, community, economic stability, the fabric of civilization."
—Russell Kirk and Historian James McClellan, *The Political Principles of Robert A. Taft*
"For his valiant effort to be in America what Churchill is to Great Britain...for the inspiration his career must be to all those who share in his patriotic aspirations—I nominate for the man of the year the late Senior Senator from the State of Ohio—Robert A. Taft."
—John F. Kennedy, quoted in *Mr. Republican: A Biography of Robert A. Taft*

making it clear that Taft could see him at any time without an appointment. The two political leaders, so different in temperament and by training, began to warm to each other. Taft's motives were a combination of the patriotic and the partisan. He told his old friend, former President Herbert Hoover, that the stakes were high for the new administration. If it did not succeed and the Republicans lost the White House in 1956, the nation and the party would go, he predicted, "into a long, long slide."[7]

Who can say what these two political giants might have forged if they had three or seven more years to work together? But in April, Taft felt a severe pain in his hip while playing golf with Ike. Less than two months later, he would announce, on crutches, that he was stepping down "temporarily" as Senate majority leader. He was fatally ill with cancer and died on July 31, 1953.

Without Taft, the dynamics of the Republican Party shifted dramatically. There was no effective counterweight to the modern Republicanism of the Eisenhower administration, which was never again as conservative as it was in the first half of 1953. And Taft would not have given McCarthy free rein to conduct the often careless senatorial inquiries in 1953 and 1954 that allowed liberals to transform anti-communism into McCarthyism and hang it around the necks of conservatives for decades.

Robert A. Taft—"Mr. Republican"—was the first founding father of the modern conservative movement. Primarily through his Senate service and leadership, Taft strengthened and shaped the conservative strain in the American character, demonstrating that prudential change was acceptable if harmonized with the historical experience of the nation. His accomplishments, Russell Kirk later wrote, were significant for the country and the movement:

- He stood for liberty under law—"the liberties of all classes of citizens, in all circumstances."
- He contended for "a humane economy" in which the benefits of American industry might be extended to every citizen.
- He fairly criticized the conduct of American foreign policy, supporting, for example, the Truman Doctrine and the Marshall Plan, but opposing NATO because of its long-term military commitments.[8]

But now Taft was gone and Douglas MacArthur had faded away, and the only remaining champion was the fiery anti-communist, Joe McCarthy. From February 1950, when he declared in a Wheeling, West Virginia, speech that communists were still employed by the State Department, until December 1954, when the U.S. Senate "condemned" his conduct, McCarthy was at the center of the American political stage. To millions, he was "Mr. Anti-Communist," a fearless prosecutor of traitors and fellow travelers. To many others, he was a reckless character assassin. A new word, "McCarthyism,"—the making of baseless accusations—was coined by his enemies. Defiant friends wore the label proudly.

McCarthy had a fatal flaw: He rarely listened to anyone, even his closest advisers, particularly when they counseled caution. Whittaker Chambers often expressed his concern about McCarthy to Bill Buckley, stating that the senator was "a slugger and a rabble-rouser" who "simply knows that somebody threw a tomato and the general direction from which it came." McCarthy, he said, had only one tactic, "attack," and that was not sufficient.[9]

THE CONSERVATIVE MIND

In the middle of the tumultuous McCarthy era, when passionate charge and countercharge filled the air, a young, unknown scholar published an intellectual history of conservative thought that permanently changed the public's perception of conservatism. Russell Kirk was only 34 in April 1953 when his seminal work, *The Conservative Mind*, appeared. Liberals at first said, condescendingly, that the title was an oxymoron, but they were forced to revise their opinion when they read Kirk's "eloquent, defiant, impassioned *cri de coeur* for conservatism."[10] It was a 450-page overview of conservative thinking in the previous 150 years and a scathing indictment of every liberal nostrum, from human perfectibility to economic egalitarianism.

Kirk declared that the essence of conservatism lay in six "canons":

1. A divine intent, as well as personal conscience, rules society;
2. Traditional life is filled with variety and mystery while most radical systems are characterized by a narrowing uniformity;
3. Civilized society requires orders and classes;
4. Property and freedom are inseparably connected;
5. Man must control his will and his appetite, knowing that he is governed more by emotion than by reason; and,
6. Society must alter slowly.[11]

The response to Kirk's monumental work was, in the words of his publisher, Henry Regnery, "beyond all expectations."[12] *The New York Times* favorably reviewed *The Conservative Mind* as did *Time*, which stated it was a "wonder of conservative intuition and prophecy."[13] Of the first 50 reviews, a majority were favorable, and with reason. *The Conservative Mind* was an impressive feat of scholarship—a synthesis of the ideas of leading conservative thinkers and political leaders of the late eighteenth through the early twentieth centuries, including Edmund Burke, John Adams, Alexis de Tocqueville, Benjamin Disraeli, Orestes Brownson, Paul Elmer More, and George Santayana. The work established convincingly that there *was* a tradition of American conservatism that had existed since the Founding. With one book, Russell Kirk made conservatism intellectually acceptable. In fact, as both Henry Regnery and William Rusher pointed out, he gave the conservative movement its name.[14]

If Kirk had done nothing else but write *The Conservative Mind*, he would have earned the enduring gratitude of every conservative. But over the following decades, Russell Kirk wrote a syndicated newspaper column that appeared in many of the nation's largest cities, provided the readers of *National Review* with his insights into higher education, and lectured and debated on hundreds of college campuses. He published over 30 books and hundreds of articles, reviews, essays, and introductions.

Twenty-one years after releasing *The Conservative Mind*, Kirk published *The Roots of American Order*, which some critics rank almost as high as the far better known *Mind*. In *Roots*, Kirk uses the geographical device of five cities to outline the ideas and institutions that nurtured the American Republic. The first roots were planted in Jerusalem with the Hebrew perception of a purposeful moral existence under God. They were strengthened in Athens by the philosophical and political self-awareness of the Greeks. They were nurtured in Rome by the Roman experience of law and social awareness. They were intertwined with the Christian understanding of human duties and human hopes, of man redeemed. They were joined by medieval custom, learning, and valor. And then these roots were enriched by two great political experiments in law and liberty in London, the mother city of parliaments, and in Philadelphia, the birthplace of the Declaration of Independence and the Constitution.

As with all of Kirk's works, *The Roots of American Order* is breathtakingly erudite, drawing on Plato, Cicero, Saint Augustine, Hobbes, Locke, John Knox, Hume, Montesquieu, Blackstone, Jonathan Edwards, Lincoln, and Orestes Brownson. It is the mature work of a master of letters.

With the publication of *The Conservative Mind* along with the earlier appearances of Hayek's *The Road to Serfdom*, Weaver's *Ideas Have Consequences*, and Chambers's *Witness*, the essential conservative canon—representing the traditional, libertarian, and anti-communist strains of conservatism—was now in place and available to popularizer, politician, and philanthropist alike.

But in the mid-1950s, conservative ideas did not seem to be taking hold in many Americans' minds. Similarly, conservative politicians found themselves far from the center of the public square. Robert Taft was dead and, after his Senate censure in December 1954, Joe McCarthy was as good as dead. President Eisenhower was offering a "dimestore" New Deal at home, while Secretary of State John Foster Dulles was accused by some conservatives of practicing chickenship rather than brinksmanship abroad.[15] When Hungarian freedom fighters rose up in October 1956, with the encouragement of the U.S.-financed Radio Free Europe, and Soviet forces invaded, the Eisenhower administration declined to act when the Soviets brutally crushed the Hungarian revolution. The GOP rested securely in the hands of Eastern Republicans who even tried to remove Vice President Nixon from the 1956 ticket because "he was not a creature of their making."[16]

The conservative movement could claim only a few publications and fewer organizations, the new youth group, the Intercollegiate Society of Individualists, being an exception. Newspaper columnists like John Chamberlain and George Sokolsky and radio broadcasters like Fulton Lewis, Jr., had their national audiences, but liberals undermined their effectiveness by usually describing them as part of the "militant right wing." CBS's Mike Wallace, for example, invited television viewers one evening to listen to Lewis explain "the attraction the far right has for crackpot fascist groups in America."[17]

Conservative victories, wrote William F. Buckley, Jr., were "uncoordinated and inconclusive" because the philosophy of freedom was not being expounded systemically in the universities and in the media. A new journal was needed to combat the liberals, compensate for "conservative weakness" in the academy, and "focus the energies" of the movement.[18] In the summer of 1954, Buckley joined forces with the German émigré William Schlamm, who had been helping to edit *The Freeman*. Both men believed that the way to change American politics was to challenge the liberal intellectuals who dominated America's ideas and that the best vehicle for doing so was a weekly intellectual magazine like the liberal *New Republic*.

With a $100,000 pledge from Buckley's father, Buckley and Schlamm wrote a prospectus to attract financial contributors and writers. They declared that the "political climate" was fashioned by serious opinion journals and it was possible to "rout intellectually" the jaded liberal status quo with the "vigor of true convictions." They described their own convictions as a synthesis of the libertarian, conservative, and anti-communist wings of American conservatism.[19] F. A. Hayek had made a similar point that the climate of public opinion was shaped by what he called the "professional second-hand dealers in ideas"—journalists, teachers, ministers, lecturers, publicists, writers, and artists.[20]

In pursuit of funds, Buckley traveled to Texas and Southern California. Oil millionaire H. L. Hunt and other members of the Texas Right found the 30-year-old Yale graduate "too Catholic, too Eastern, and too moderate."[21] The young fundraiser encountered more congenial conservatives in the Golden State, several of them through the Hollywood writer Morrie Ryskind, an outspoken anti-communist who had written most of the Marx Brothers' movies and had won a Pulitzer Prize for the book of the Gershwins' musical satire, *Of Thee I Sing.* By September 1955, with the help of Yale alumni like South Carolina textile manufacturer Roger Milliken and New York financier Jeremiah Milbank, Jr., Buckley had raised about $300,000. His goal had been $450,000 to meet the anticipated deficits of the first two years. When the young editor hesitated, Schlamm was adamant that they go ahead. "Willi's point," Buckley recalled, "was that if you get twenty-five thousand readers, your subscribers won't let you die, and that proved almost exactly accurate."[22]

Buckley welded an impressive, broad-based intellectual coalition. On the masthead and among its writers were traditionalists Russell Kirk and Richard Weaver, libertarians John Chamberlain and Frank Chodorov, and anti-communists James Burnham and Frank Meyer. The editors declared themselves to be "irrevocably" at war with "satanic" communism; described the central crisis of the era as the conflict between the "Social Engineers" and the "disciples of Truth, who defend the organic moral order"; and joined with the "libertarian side" in the battle against "the growth of government."[23]

In the first issue, Buckley sounded the clarion, averring that conservatives lived, as did all other Americans, in "a Liberal world." *National Review* would not submit but would stand "athwart history yelling Stop," confident that "a vigorous and incorruptible journal of conservative opinion" could make a critical difference in the realms of ideas and politics.[24] *National Review* was not just a journal of opinion but a deliberate political act, one of a handful that shaped the modern American conservative movement in the post–World War II period.

AN UNLIKELY REVOLUTIONARY

At the same time, a new political star was rising in the West. Barry Goldwater was the grandson of a Jewish peddler who became a millionaire; a college dropout whose book *The Conscience of a Conservative* would sell 3.5 million copies (it was for a while required reading for History 169B at Harvard University). He delighted in challenging conventional wisdom but always used the Constitution as his guide. He insisted that doing something about the farm problem "means—and there can be no equivocation here—prompt and final termination of the farm subsidy program." He declared that welfare ought to be "a private concern . . . promoted by individuals and families, by churches, private hospitals, religious service organizations, community charities, and other institutions."[25] In his political manifesto, *The Conscience of a Conservative*, Goldwater said the future of freedom depended upon the election of public officials who pledged to enforce the Constitution and who proclaimed: "My aim is not to pass laws, but to repeal them."[26]

When *The Conscience of a Conservative* (ghostwritten by L. Brent Bozell, who had been the senator's speechwriter) was published in April 1960, it was a political sensation, creating a new national spokesman and proclaiming a major new force in national politics—conservatism. *The Chicago Tribune's* George Morgenstern declared that there was "more harsh fact and hard sense in this slight book than will emerge from all of the chatter of this year's session of Congress [and] this year's campaign for the presidency." Veteran columnist Westbrook Pegler wrote perceptively that "Senator Barry Goldwater of Arizona certainly is now the successor to Senator Taft of Ohio as defender of the Constitution and freedom."[27]

All the ingredients of a national political movement were coming together: a charismatic political leader, Barry Goldwater; widely known popularizers young (Bill Buckley) and old (George

Sokolsky); thinkers like Hayek, Kirk, and Friedman in their intellectual prime; and far-sighted "golden" donors like J. Howard Pew and Roger Milliken. Movement leaders now decided they required an organization of young activists who would serve as the ground troops of conservatism in the coming battles. And so in the fall of 1960, some 90 young conservatives met at the Sharm, Connecticut, home of Bill Buckley and founded Young Americans for Freedom, with a little help from older Americans for freedom like Buckley, William A. Rusher, and organizational guru Marvin Liebman. They elected as their first president the brilliant, irreverent and Jewish Robert M. Schuchman of Yale. Douglas Caddy, a Catholic graduate of Georgetown University, was named executive director. They also adopted the Sharon Statement, drafted by 26-year-old M. Stanton Evans (editor of the *Indianapolis News*), which affirmed certain truths at "this time of moral and political crisis," especially: "Foremost among the transcendent values is the individual's use of his God-given free will, whence derives his right to be free from the restrictions of arbitrary force."[28]

The Sharon Statement was a succinct summary of the central ideas of modern American conservatism: Free will and moral authority come from God; political and economic liberty are essential for a free people and free institutions; government must be strictly and constitutionally limited; the market economy is the economic system most compatible with freedom; and communism must be defeated, not simply contained.

Young Americans for Freedom (YAF) went on to serve the conservative movement throughout the 1960s, providing the National Draft Goldwater Committee with critical manpower in a dozen states; challenging the liberal agenda of the National Student Association on 100 college campuses; supporting American servicemen in Vietnam through "bleed-ins" (blood donations), debates,

Richard Weaver

(Born March 3, 1910; died April 3, 1963)

A brilliant but reclusive professor of English at the University of Chicago, Richard Weaver challenged the liberal ideas that threatened the foundations of Western civilization with powerful works like *Ideas Have Consequences* and *The Ethics of Rhetoric*. Obtaining degrees from the University of Kentucky, Vanderbilt University and Louisiana State University, Weaver served as a contributing editor for *National Review* and *Modern Age* as well as a trustee for the Intercollegiate Society of Individualists, now the Intercollegiate Studies Institute.

SELECTED WRITINGS

Ideas Have Consequences, 1948

The Ethics of Rhetoric, 1953

Visions of Order: The Cultural Crisis of Our Time, 1964

RECOMMENDED AUTOBIOGRAPHICAL ESSAY

"Up from Liberalism," *Life Without Prejudice and Other Essays*, Richard Weaver, Regnery Publishers, 1965

NOTABLE QUOTE

"For four centuries every man has been...his own professor of ethics, and the consequence is an anarchy which threatens even that minimum consensus of value necessary to the political state."

—*Ideas Have Consequences*

THE DIFFERENCE HE MADE

"*Ideas Have Consequences* is the *fons et origo* [source and origin] of the contemporary American conservative movement."

—Frank S. Meyer, quoted in George Nash, *The Conservative Intellectual Movement in America Since 1945*

"Weaver had sowed deep his intellectual seed, and although he left no heirs of his body, the heirs of his mind may be many and stalwart."

—Russell Kirk, *The Sword of Imagination*

and symposia; and even picketing the Firestone Tire and Rubber Company when it tried to build a synthetic rubber plant in communist Romania.

Like the editors of *National Review*, YAF members were divided over the right course of action in the Kennedy–Nixon presidential race in November 1960. Realist James Burnham favored an endorsement of Nixon, while political strategist Bill Rusher argued that a vote for Nixon would "enhance" the liberal management of the Republican Party.[29] Goldwater did not share the satisfaction of some hard-core conservatives when Nixon was defeated, but he did argue that the vice president and his patrician running mate, Henry Cabot Lodge, had failed to give the voters a "clear-cut choice." They narrowly lost, he said, "because [they] were not Republican enough."[30] If he ever ran for president, Goldwater vowed, he would campaign as a traditional Republican and conservative without apology. He quickly added when asked about the 1964 presidential race, "I have no staff for it, no program for it, and no ambition for it."[31] But others had enough of all three for him.

THE RELUCTANT CHAMPION

Three young but politically experienced conservatives recognized Goldwater's enormous political potential and created "the first authentic presidential nomination draft in the history of American political parties."[32] The three close friends and former leaders of the Young Republicans, were William A. Rusher, the strategist, who had served in World War II and then graduated from Harvard Law School before becoming a kingmaker (and breaker) in the Young Republicans and Young Americans for Freedom; F. Clifton White, the tactician, a tall, bow-tied professional politician from New York who had taught politics at Cornell and then worked in the presidential campaigns of Dewey,

Eisenhower, and Nixon; and Congressman John M. Ashbrook of Ohio, the ideologue and former chairman of the Young Republican National Federation.

Rusher, White, and Ashbrook combined their skills in organizing, fundraising, and public relations to create the National Draft Goldwater Committee, which by mid-November 1963 had persuaded Barry Goldwater he ought to announce his candidacy for the Republican nomination for president and challenge John Kennedy in the 1964 election. Goldwater had been initially reluctant because he wanted to remain in the Senate where he was comfortable and effective, because he had real doubts about his intellectual ability to be president (he once told a reporter he did not have a first-class brain), and because all the polls showed him losing to President Kennedy. But the draft committee's energetic grassroots efforts and impressive fundraising (led by New Yorkers J. William Middendorf II and Jeremiah Milbank, Jr.) helped to convince him that he had an excellent chance of winning the nomination and making a respectable showing against the incumbent president.

While the politicians, led by Clif White, were busy building a national organization to gain the presidential nomination for their hesitant champion, the popularizers, led by *National Review*, were busily removing extremist elements from the movement. Several years earlier, Whittaker Chambers had taken up arms against Ayn Rand, the neo-Nietzschean founder of objectivism, and her 1,168-page novel *Atlas Shrugged*. Writing in *National Review*, Chambers declared that its story was preposterous, its characters cruel caricatures, and its message "dictatorial." Although Rand insisted she was anti-statist, Chambers said, she called for a society run by a "technocratic elite." "Out of a lifetime of reading," he wrote, "I can recall no other book in which a tone of overriding arrogance was so irrevocably sustained."[33]

As conservatism became a meaningful presence in American politics, liberals began seeking ways to limit its effectiveness. They decided to attack the conservative movement at a vulnerable point— the ultra-right John Birch Society. President Kennedy delivered a major speech in the fall of 1961 in which he urged Americans to reject "fanatics" who found "treason" everywhere and did not trust the people. Although Kennedy did not name the "fanatics," *The New York Times* obligingly did so in a front-page story, mentioning the John Birch Society and the paramilitary Minutemen.[34]

Over the objections of Bill Rusher, Frank Meyer, and new senior editor William Rickenbacker (son of the legendary World War I ace, Captain Eddie Rickenbacker), Bill Buckley, supported by his sister and managing editor Priscilla and James Burnham, wrote a powerful editorial in February 1962, reading John Birch Society founder Robert Welch out of the conservative movement. Noting the criticism of Welch by such staunch anti-communists as Barry Goldwater, Walter H. Judd, Fulton Lewis, Jr., and Russell Kirk, the *National Review* editorial concluded that a love of truth and country called for the firm rejection of Welch's "false counsels." (Among other deliriums, Welch's annual scoreboard described the United States of America as "50–70 percent Communist-controlled.")[35]

One other important task had to be accomplished before the conservative movement could operate effectively in the political realm: It had to be philosophically united. Traditionalists and libertarians had been snapping and snarling at each other in the pages of *National Review* and elsewhere. One conservative in particular was convinced that beneath all the supposed differences lay a consensus of principle: Frank Meyer, the fast-talking, chain-smoking, ex-communist senior editor of *National Review*. Through articles, books, and countless post-midnight telephone calls, Meyer communicated his synthesis of the differing elements of conservatism, which came to be called *fusionism*.

The core principle of fusionism was that "the freedom of the person [is] the central and primary end of political society." The state had only three limited functions: national defense, the preservation of domestic order, and the administration of justice between citizens. The "achievement of virtue" was not the state's business. Freedom, Meyer argued, was the indispensable condition for the pursuit of virtue. And yet he insisted that modern American conservatism was not classical liberalism, which had been significantly weakened by utilitarianism and secularism. Conservatives sought to save the Christian understanding of "the nature and destiny of man." To do that, they had to absorb the best of both branches of the divided conservative mainstream. Meyer insisted he was not creating anything new, but rather articulating an already existing conservative consensus—"the consensus forged so brilliantly by the Founding Fathers in 1789" at the writing of the Constitution.[36]

From the mid-50s until his death in 1972, Frank Meyer was "a central and unifying figure," to quote M. Stanton Evans, in the largely successful effort to bridge the philosophical divide between traditionalists and libertarians. Meyer argued that religious and traditional precepts were needed to undergird freedom, which could not exist on the relativist–materialistic premises of modern thought. At the same time, liberty was linked to American religion because it was the source of ethical choice and was "a unique by-product of Western faith." Practically speaking, Evans points out, Meyer was arguing that "the conservative movement *was* a movement," not a jumble of factions. And as a movement it could go forth "to smite the liberal-Left behemoth."[37]

Although both traditionalists and libertarians often challenged fusionism in the years to come, it prevailed as an effective synthesis until the collapse of communism in Eastern and Central Europe in

1989 and the dissolution of the Soviet Union in 1991. And without a united conservative movement behind him, Barry Goldwater would not have been nominated for president in 1964. Indeed, Goldwater was the embodiment of fusionism in his presidential campaign, stressing the need for morality in government, lamenting a national decline in law and order, promising less government and more individual freedom, and calling for victory over the Soviet Union in the Cold War.

Movement Builders

1 Phyllis Schlafly, *A Choice Not an Echo* (Alton, Illinois: Pere Marquette, 1964), p. 58.

2 William Manchester, *The Glory and the Dream: A Narrative History of America, 1932–1972*, Vol. I (Boston: Little, Brown and Company, 1973), p. 756.

3 "The Problem of Taft," *Human Events*, November 7, 1951, p. 399.

4 William S. White, *The Taft Story* (New York: Harper & Brothers, 1954), p. 181.

5 Arthur Krock column, *The New York Times*, November 5, 1952.

6 James T. Patterson, *Grand Expectations: The United States, 1945–1974* (New York: Oxford University Press, 1996), p. 279.

7 White, *The Taft Story*, p. 251.

8 Kirk and McClellan, *The Political Principles of Robert A. Taft*, p. 195.

9 Nash, *The Conservative Intellectual Movement in America Since 1945*, pp. 114–115.

10 *Ibid.*, p. 73.

11 Russell Kirk, *The Conservative Mind from Burke to Santayana*, rev. ed. (Chicago: Henry Regnery and Company, 1953), pp. 7–8.

12 Nash, *The Conservative Intellectual Movement in America Since 1945*, p. 73.

13 "Generation to Generation," *Time*, July 6, 1953.

14 Henry Regnery, "A Conservative Publisher in a Liberal World," *The Alternative*, October 1971, pp. 14–16, and William Rusher, "Death of a Giant," *University Bookman* 34, 1994, p.16.

15 See Lee Edwards, *Goldwater: The Man Who Made a Revolution* (Washington, D.C.: Regnery Publishing, Inc., 1995), p. 324.

16 Schlafly, *A Choice Not an Echo*, p. 69.

17 "Mike Wallace Interviews Fulton Lewis Jr.," February 1, 1958, Post-Presidential File: Fulton Lewis, Jr., Herbert Hoover Presidential Library, West Branch, Iowa.

18 Nash, *The Conservative Intellectual Movement in America Since 1945*, pp. 140–141.

19 John B. Judis, *William F. Buckley Jr.: Patron Saint of the Conservatives* (New York: Simon and Schuster, 1988), p. 119.

20 See Friedrich A. Hayek, "The Intellectuals and Socialism:" First published in the *University of Chicago Law Review*, Vol. 16, No. 3, Spring 1949, and reprinted by the Institute of Economic Analysis in 1998 as No. 4 in its Rediscovered Riches series.

[21] Judis, *William F. Buckley Jr.*, p. 120.

[22] *Ibid.*, p. 129.

[23] "The Magazine's Credenda," *National Review*, November 19, 1955, p. 6.

[24] *Ibid.*, p. 5.

[25] Barry Goldwater, *The Conscience of a Conservative* (Shepherdsville, Ky.: Victor Publishing Company, 1960), pp. 42, 74.

[26] *Ibid.*, p. 17.

[27] George Mortenstern, "Harsh Facts, Hard Sense on the Perils to Liberty," *Chicago Sunday Tribune Magazine of Books*, April 17, 1960; "Old Guard's New Spokesman," *Time*, May 2, 1960; Westbrook Pegler, "The Conscience of a Conservative," *New York Journal American*, April 29, 1960.

[28] Lee Edwards, *You Can Make the Difference* (New Rochelle, N.Y.: Arlington House, 1980), pp. 241–242.

[29] William A. Rusher to William F. Buckley, Jr., October 10, 1960, in Buckley Papers, Sterling Library, Yale University.

[30] Barry Goldwater, *With No Apologies* (New York: William Morrow and Company, 1979), p. 125.

[31] "Salesman for a Cause," *Time*, June 23, 1961, p. 16.

[32] F. Clifton White with William J. Gill, *Suite 3505: The Story of the Draft Goldwater Movement* (New Rochelle, N.Y.: Arlington House, 1967), p. 35.

[33] Whittaker Chambers, "Big Sister Is Watching You," *National Review*, December 28, 1957, pp. 594–596.

[34] William A. Rusher, *The Rise of the Right* (New York: William Morrow and Company, 1984), pp. 121–123.

[35] "The Question of Robert Welch," *National Review*, February 13, 1962, pp. 83–88.

[36] Nash, *The Conservative Intellectual Movement in America Since 1945*, p. 161.

[37] M. Stanton Evans, foreword by Kevin J. Smart, *Principles and Heresies: Frank S. Meyer and the Shaping of the American Conservative Movement* (Wilmington, Del.: ISI Books, 2002), pp. xv–xvi.

Chapter 3

Principled Politicians

A CHOICE NOT AN ECHO

The rising fortunes of the conservative movement and its no longer reluctant champion were confirmed by several major events in the summer and fall of 1963. Eight thousand ecstatic conservatives jammed Washington's National Guard Armory on the Fourth of July to persuade Barry Goldwater to lead a crusade to make America strong again. Nearly 50,000 people filled Dodger Stadium in Los Angeles to hear Goldwater deliver a speech that was interrupted 47 times as he declared that "America needs a change" and "Freedom needs a chance."[1]

These were heady times for Goldwater and the conservative movement capped by a major article in *Time* that reported "a state-by-state survey of *Time* correspondents indicates that at least Republican Barry Goldwater could give [President] Kennedy a breathlessly close contest."[2] As November drew to a close, Barry Goldwater was convinced he could run a strong, principled campaign against an incumbent liberal president. The American conservative movement was prepared to help him capture the Republican presidential nomination and then, perhaps, the most sought-after prize in American politics—the presidency. Then, on Friday, November 22, 1963, a smiling, sun-tanned President

Kennedy settled back in an open limousine to parade through downtown Dallas.

The bullet that killed John F. Kennedy also killed Barry Goldwater's chances to become president. The American people did not want three different presidents in a single year. And yet the Arizona conservative still announced his candidacy for the Republican nomination, unwilling to disappoint the millions who looked to him as a political savior. Rarely does a presidential candidate run knowing beyond a reasonable doubt that he cannot win. That hard political reality accounted for Goldwater's grim face throughout 1964 (no one enjoys committing political suicide), and the uncompromising contents of his speeches and positions (he would give the voters a *real* choice).

Goldwater could depend on something that heretofore had not existed—a national political movement. Although untested in a national campaign, conservatism did have a clearly defined, consistent philosophy, as articulated by Hayek, Weaver, Chambers, and Kirk; an expanding national constituency, particularly strong in the West and the South; a charismatic, nationally known leader; and a solid financial base, not dependent on a few wealthy individuals but on thousands of grassroots supporters who had contributed to the National Draft Goldwater Committee. In the mass media, however, conservative ideas and spokesmen confronted a largely skeptical and even hostile body.

Although the favorite in early GOP polling, Goldwater lost the March Republican primary in New Hampshire primarily because of his careless rhetoric—saying, for example, that the NATO commander should have the ability to use tactical "nuclear weapons." That was, in fact, long-standing NATO policy in certain crisis situations, but New York Governor Nelson Rockefeller immediately charged that Goldwater wanted to turn over the authority to use theater nuclear weapons to *all* commanders in the field. Thus was created the image of "Goldwater the Trigger-Happy Warrior."[3]

With any other candidate, Goldwater's poor New Hampshire showing (he finished a distant second to write-in candidate Henry Cabot Lodge) would have seriously damaged him. But, in 1964, the county and state conventions rather than the primaries were the key to the Republican nomination. Because of the groundwork done by Clif White and the Draft Goldwater Committee, Goldwater picked up 48 delegates the same day he lost New Hampshire and kept on accumulating delegates in state after state. By mid-May, the senator was well on his way to capturing the 655 votes necessary for nomination. But first came California.

The California primary between Barry Goldwater and Nelson Rockefeller was the most consequential in the history of the American conservative movement. It was an epic battle between Goldwater volunteers and Rockefeller mercenaries, the New Right and the old California establishment, the man who did not really want to be president and the man who wanted only to be president. A Goldwater army of as many as 50,000 (the largest number of volunteer workers ever assembled for any presidential primary before or since) distributed literature, canvassed neighborhoods, and prepared to get Goldwater voters to the polls. One of the most effective pieces of literature was Phyllis Schlafly's anti-establishment paperback, *A Choice Not an Echo*; an estimated half-million copies of the Schlafly tract were distributed throughout the state. Rockefeller countered with a tidal wave of scurrilous brochures and pamphlets that pictured Goldwater as an isolated extremist who would drop the H–bomb if he were elected. The attacks backfired, inspiring Goldwater supporters to work all the harder and forcing other Republican leaders to deny they were part of any anti-Goldwater effort.

On June 2, a red-letter day in American conservatism, Goldwater edged Rockefeller by 68,350 votes out of 2.2 million cast—51.6

percent of the total. If Goldwater had lost California, he might have withdrawn from the race or been denied the nomination, although Clif White argued that the Goldwater delegates would not bolt. Republican liberals would have united behind Rockefeller and done whatever was necessary to defeat conservatives at the national convention, as they had in 1940, 1948, and 1952. But by winning California, Goldwater demonstrated his popular appeal as well as his organizational skill. His nomination was now inevitable, although liberals persuaded Pennsylvania Governor William Scranton to mount an 11th-hour challenge. Scranton's fruitless campaign served only to divide Republicans and give Democrats the theme of extremism they would use so effectively in the general election.

When former President Eisenhower expressed his approval of the Republican platform (drafted by conservatives) and said that if Goldwater campaigned on it, "I don't see how he can go far wrong," the anti-Goldwater cabal produced the infamous "Scranton letter." The 1,200-word screed called the senator the leader of radical extremists and "Goldwaterism" a collection of "absurd and dangerous positions." It spitefully described Goldwater's positions as irresponsible, right-wing, extremist, racist, and a "crazy-quilt collection" that would be "soundly repudiated by the American people in November."[4]

The letter failed to shake the steady resolve of the Republican delegates to nominate Barry Goldwater for president, but it provoked the nominee into delivering the most controversial acceptance speech in the history of national conventions, rivaled only by William Jennings Bryan's famous "cross of gold" address in 1896. The Goldwater team offered no olive branch to the vanquished liberals, regarding the senator's nomination as an opportunity to signal that conservatives intended to set "a new course in GOP national politics."[5] The designated speechwriter was not Karl Hess, the senator's usual scribe, but Harry Jaffa, a Lincoln scholar and professor of political science at Ohio State University, whose memorandum on extremism, written for the platform hearings, had impressed Goldwater.

In his speech, Goldwater borrowed freely from the Old Testament, warning the American people they had been following "false prophets" and exhorting them to return to "proven ways—not because they are old but because they are true." He stated that Americans "must, and we shall, set the tide running again in the cause of freedom."[6] As he neared the conclusion of his acceptance address, Goldwater called for a "focused" and "dedicated" Republicanism that rejected "unthinking and stupid labels." The next lines were underlined in the original text:

I would remind you that extremism in the defense of liberty is no vice!

And let me remind you also that moderation in the pursuit of justice is no virtue![7]

Conservatives roared their approval, liberals turned red in the face, moderates blanched, and a reporter blurted, "My God, he's going to run as Barry Goldwater."[8] Indeed he was, knowing he had as much chance of defeating President Johnson as Billy Graham had of being elected pope. The night before, Goldwater had seen a national survey by his own pollster showing LBJ leading him by nearly three to one, a margin that no politician realistically could be expected to overcome. But with Goldwater's nomination, control of the Republican Party passed to the conservatives.

LANDSLIDE

President Johnson was determined to win by the largest landslide ever, eclipsing the historic victory of his political idol Franklin D. Roosevelt over the hapless Alf Landon in 1936. For Johnson, extremism in the pursuit of the presidency was no vice.

He filled his speeches with warnings about the danger of voting for an extremist. He played on the public's fear of nuclear war. He contrasted Goldwater's "intention" to eliminate Social Security, the Tennessee Valley Authority, and other federal programs with his own commitment to a Great Society in which every American, particularly the underprivileged, would have "a larger share of the growing pie."[9]

Johnson directed his aide Bill Moyers to "remind people of what Barry Goldwater was before he was nominated for president" and began trying to shed "the extremism that surrounded him all of his career."[10] Moyers passed the word to the Democrats' advertising agency, which disgorged one of the most negative ad campaigns in national politics. The most damaging spot was the "Daisy" commercial in which the camera opened on a little girl standing in a field and picking petals from a daisy. Suddenly an ominous voice started counting down from 10 to zero. At "zero," the camera dissolved from the pupil of the child's eye to the mushroom cloud of an exploding atomic bomb. Johnson's voice said solemnly, "These are the stakes—to make a world in which all of God's children can live, or to go into the dark. We must either love each other, or we must die." An announcer repeated the words that appeared in white on a black screen, "Vote for President Johnson on November 3. The stakes are too high for you to stay home."[11]

In a different political climate, this apocalyptic approach might have invoked disbelief or even laughter, but as a result of unremitting political attacks and the anti-Goldwater bias of the mass media, millions of Americans believed that a President Goldwater would bring about a nuclear holocaust. Fueling voters' intense fears were articles like the cover article in *Fact* magazine that trumpeted in large black letters: "1,189 Psychiatrists Say Goldwater Is Psychologically Unfit to Be President." Some of the more partisan psychiatrists

William F. Buckley Jr.

(Born November 24, 1925)

As founder and editor in chief of *National Review*, syndicated columnist, host of *Firing Line* (public TV's longest-running weekly program), author of more than 40 books, and college lecturer for over five decades, Bill Buckley has been the renaissance man of the modern American conservative movement. A graduate of Yale University, Buckley has been published in a wide variety of publications ranging from *Architectural Digest* to *Saturday Review*. Buckley is the recipient of numerous awards including Best Columnist of the Year, 1967, the Presidential Medal of Freedom, 1991, and The Heritage Foundation's Clare Boothe Luce Award, 1999.

CAREER

Founding president, Intercollegiate Society of Individualists, 1953

Founder, *National Review*, 1955

Co-founder, New York Conservative Party, 1961

Mayoral candidate, New York City, 1965

Host, *Firing Line*, 1966–2000

Delegate to the United Nations, 1973

Syndicated columnist, 1962–present

SELECTED WRITINGS

God and Man at Yale, 1951

McCarthy and His Enemies, 1954

Up From Liberalism, 1959

Did You Ever See a Dream Walking? American Conservative Thought in the Twentieth Century, 1970

Saving the Queen, 1976

Mongoose, R.I.P., 1987

Nearer, My God, 1997

Getting It Right, 2003

The Fall of the Berlin Wall, 2004

Miles Gone By, 2004

RECOMMENDED BIOGRAPHY

William F. Buckley Jr.: Patron Saint of the Conservatives, John B. Judis, Simon & Schuster, 1988.

NOTABLE QUOTE

"I am obliged to confess that I should sooner live in a society governed by the first two thousand names in the Boston telephone directory than in a society governed by the first two thousand faculty members of Harvard University."

—*Rumbles Left and Right*

THE DIFFERENCE HE MADE

"[William F. Buckley, Jr.] didn't just part the Red Sea—[he] rolled it back, dried it up, and left exposed, for all the world to see, the naked desert that is statism."

—Ronald Reagan, quoted in *William F. Buckley Jr.: Patron Saint of the Conservatives*

"And before there was Ronald Reagan, there was Barry Goldwater, and before there was Barry Goldwater, there was *National Review*, and before there was *National Review*, there was Bill Buckley with a spark in his mind, and the spark in 1980 became a conflagration."

—Columnist George Will, *National Review*, December 31, 1980

"The history of reflective conservatism in America after 1955 is the history of the individuals who collaborated in—or were discovered by—the magazine William F. Buckley Jr. founded."

—Historian George H. Nash, *The Conservative Intellectual Movement in America Since 1945*

compared Goldwater with Hitler and Stalin and called him "a mass murderer at heart."[12] The White House also approved a radio commercial that shattered the truth-in-advertising record by asserting, "Barry Goldwater's plan means the end of Social Security, the end of widows' pensions, the end of the dignity that comes with being able to take care of yourself without depending on your children."[13]

In response to what he called "electronic dirt," Goldwater explained over and over that, far from wrecking the system, he had voted for every Social Security measure that had ever come before the Senate.[14] It did not make any difference. During the primaries, liberal Republicans had created a cruel caricature of Goldwater and Democrats reproduced it in every available medium, spurred on by an obsessed president.

Convinced of Goldwater's certain defeat and concerned about a demoralization of the conservative movement that might ensue, Bill Buckley, as the unofficial guardian of the movement, gave two unusual campaign speeches that fall: one at the annual convention of Young Americans for Freedom and the other at the anniversary dinner of the New York Conservative Party. YAF leaders wanted to fire up their members for the campaign, but Buckley talked about Goldwater's "impending defeat." As young men and women openly wept, Buckley explained that Goldwater's election would "pre-suppose a sea change in American public opinion" but the tide was still going in the other (and liberal) direction. The point of the campaign, he insisted, was not to gain victory on November 3 but to "win recruits" for "future Novembers."[15] YAF officials were so stunned they did not publish Buckley's address until after the election.

At the Conservative Party dinner, Buckley barely mentioned Goldwater but devoted himself to discussing conservatism's future. He confessed his surprise that the movement, confronted as it was by "the contrary tug of history," had advanced as far as it had. But, he said, there was in America a growing "spirit of resistance" to the fruits of liberalism. The challenge for conservative politics, he argued, was to "mediate between the ideal and the prudential."[16] The question of how best to balance the ideal and the prudential would preoccupy conservative leaders from Ronald Reagan to Newt Gingrich to George W. Bush for the next 40 years.

A clumsy attempt by Goldwater's campaign managers to be "prudential" almost led to the cancellation of what the senator himself called "the best speech of the campaign"—Ronald Reagan's nationally televised address, "A Time for Choosing." Advisers, led by unofficial campaign manager William Baroody, Sr., were worried about references in Reagan's talk to Social Security and his suggestion of a voluntary option. Goldwater personally reviewed the Reagan speech, essentially the one the Hollywood actor had given from 1954 to 1962 as a spokesman for General Electric. "What the hell's wrong with that?" Goldwater asked and gave the go-ahead for a 30-minute, black-and-white TV program (aired on October 27, 1964) that made political history.[17]

America had come, Reagan said, to "a time for choosing" between free enterprise and big government—between individual liberty and "the ant heap of totalitarianism." Borrowing language from the Democratic president for whom he had cast his first vote in 1932, Reagan concluded:

> You and I have a rendezvous with destiny. We can preserve for our children this the last best hope of man on earth or we can sentence them to take the first step into a thousand years of darkness. If we fail, at least let our children and our children's children say of us, we justified our brief moment here. We did all that could be done.[18]

Political analysts David Broder and Stephen Hess called the Reagan speech "the most successful national political debut since William Jennings Bryan electrified the 1896 Democratic convention."[19] Businessman Henry Salvatori said that he and other leading California Republicans would not have approached Reagan to run for governor of their state had it not been for "A Time for Choosing."[20] The speech raised several million dollars from constant rebroadcasts in the following week and switched tens of thousands of votes. But President Johnson still got his historic landslide, receiving more than 43 million votes to Goldwater's 27 million. His 61 percent of the popular vote topped the record set by FDR in 1936. Goldwater won just six states—the deep South of Alabama, Georgia, Mississippi, Louisiana, and South Carolina, and his home state of Arizona.

Liberal commentators declared that the conservative movement was dead. Walter Lippmann, the king of the columnists, opined that "the Johnson victory is indisputable proof that the voters are in the center." Richard Rovere argued in *Commentary* that "the election had finished the Goldwater school of political reaction." James Reston, Washington bureau chief of *The New York Times*, concluded that "Barry Goldwater not only lost the presidential election yesterday but the conservative cause as well."[21]

Conservatives emphatically disagreed. "A party that polls over [27] million votes," said former Senator William Knowland, "is neither bankrupt nor on its deathbed." "The landslide majority did not vote against the conservative philosophy," wrote Ronald Reagan, "they voted against a false image our liberal opponents successfully mounted." Frank Meyer pointed out that despite the liberal campaign to make conservatism seem "extremist, radical, nihilist, anarchic," two-fifths of the voters still voted for the conservative alternative. "Conservatives," Meyer insisted, "stand today nearer to victory than they ever have since Franklin Roosevelt." *Human Events* stated that the Goldwater campaign had accomplished three critical things: "The Republican party is essentially conservative; the South is developing into a major pivot of its power; and a candidate who possesses Goldwater's virtues but lacks some of his handicaps can win the presidency."[22]

Even on the Left some disputed the Lippmann–Rovere–Reston thesis that conservatism was dead. In the *Nation*, Hollywood Ten alumnus Dalton Trumbo pointed out that never before had "a candidate of the right been so attractive, or aroused such profound devotion." Far from being interred, Trumbo lamented, the conservative movement was exhibiting "vigor and variety and burgeoning health."[23] Indeed it was. Among the new post–1964 organizations of the movement were the American Conservative Union, a lobbying organization; the Free Society, a think tank; the Conservative Book Club and its sister publisher, Arlington House; and the Philadelphia Society, a group of conservative intellectuals patterned after the Mont Pelerin Society.

One of the most important legacies of the Goldwater campaign was the use of direct mail to raise funds for a candidate or cause and at the same time to educate the recipient about that candidate or cause. The technique was perfected by Richard A. Viguerie, dubbed the "funding father" of the conservative movement by conservative activist Morton Blackwell. Like other young conservatives, the 31-year-old Viguerie had been shocked by the magnitude of Goldwater's loss, but he saw a golden opportunity in the failed campaign that no one else recognized. He went to the office of the clerk of the House of Representatives, which had on file the names and addresses of all those who had given $50 or more to Goldwater. Viguerie copied down their names and addresses by hand "until my fingers were numb" and then hired several others to finish the job.[24] He wound up with 12,500 conservative donors, the genesis of a list that would eventually grow into the millions.

Over the next quarter of a century, Richard Viguerie helped finance dozens of political candidates (including Republican Congressman John Ashbrook's challenge of President Nixon in 1972) and as many conservative organizations; refined the use of letters as means of informing and motivating people; trained young men and women in the art of direct mail (many of whom now head their own marketing companies); brought key conservatives together at countless breakfasts, luncheons, and dinners to advance conservatism and confound liberalism; and helped found the New Right.

One liberal who understood very well that Goldwater was not just another also-ran was the historian Theodore White. "Again and again in American history," White wrote, "it has happened that the losers of the presidency contributed almost as much to the permanent tone and dialogue of politics as did the winners."[25] Goldwater was in fact the most important loser in modern presidential politics.

He was, to begin with, the first presidential nominee to run openly as a conservative. Indeed, he was not so much the nominee of a political party as the personification of a political movement. With his grassroots appeal, Goldwater helped the Republican Party to broaden its financial base by a factor of 30 to one, with the number of individual contributors to his campaign topping 650,000. Thousands of young people entered—and stayed in—politics because of Barry Goldwater. Those young conservatives now sit in Congress and on the Supreme Court, manage campaigns and raise millions of dollars, head think tanks and write seminal books, edit magazines, and anchor radio and television programs. Barry Goldwater addressed in a serious and substantive way the issues that have dominated the national debate ever since—Social Security, government subsidies, privatization, morality in government, and communism. Campaign strategist John Sears argued that Goldwater changed "the rhetoric of politics" by challenging the principles of the New Deal, "something no Democrat or Republican before him had dared to do."[26]

There were several milestones in the first 20 years of the conservative movement including the founding of the Mont Pelerin Society; the conviction of Alger Hiss; the publication of *The Conservative Mind*; the birth of *National Review*; the launching of Young Americans for Freedom. But none equaled the political importance of Barry Goldwater's seemingly quixotic run for the White House. His candidacy was, as commentator and sometime presidential candidate

Patrick Buchanan said, "like a first love" for countless young men and women, never to be forgotten, always to be cherished. It was the beginning rather than the end of conservatism's political ascendancy.[27]

THE CITIZEN POLITICIAN

While President Johnson was preparing to implement the Great Society, a man who had never run for public office was preparing to offer the people a different kind of society, a "creative society," that would reduce the size and burden of government and make the man in the street feel that he could make a difference in what was going on around him. Ronald Reagan spent most of 1965 determining whether the ordinary citizen of California as well as the professional Republican wanted him to run for governor of the second most populous state in the union. Once satisfied there was broad-based bi-partisan support for his entry, Reagan declared his candidacy and quickly demonstrated that he was a natural on the campaign trial.

In June 1966, he won the GOP nomination by better than two to one, carrying 53 of California's 58 counties. In November, he trounced incumbent Democratic Governor Edmund "Pat" Brown by one million votes. With Reagan at the head of the ticket, Republicans won every major state office but one and made substantial gains in the state assembly and senate. By the following July, after only six months as governor, Reagan was ranked in opinion polls as a serious contender for the Republican presidential nomination, running ahead of the perennial liberal candidate, Governor Nelson Rockefeller of New York.

But the favorite of Republicans in 1968 was Richard Nixon, who, understanding where the political power of the party rested, systematically courted and enlisted conservatives in his cause. Nevertheless, Reagan declared his candidacy on the eve of the Republican convention, on the assumption that if Nixon did not win on the first ballot his delegate total would shrink on succeeding ballots like "a scoop of ice cream in the sun."[28] But Reagan and his supporters had not included in their calculations Barry Goldwater as well as Senators Strom Thurmond of South Carolina and John Tower of Texas, who "shored the Southern dike against Reagan's rising waters."[29] When Wisconsin put Nixon over the top on the first ballot, Reagan made his way to the rostrum to make the nomination unanimous. But Reagan and the conservatives had had their impact: They persuaded Nixon to accept a right-of-center platform and pick a vice presidential candidate, Governor Spiro Agnew of Maryland, who became a conservative favorite.

Facing Vice President Hubert Humphrey, an old-line liberal Democrat, Nixon steered right in the fall campaign on most issues. How different the nation and the rest of the world would have been if Nixon had delivered on the limited government, anti-communist promises he made to the American electorate in the fall of 1968. Instead, from almost his first day in office, Nixon offered a pseudo-New Deal at home and an accommodationist foreign policy abroad. And he closed himself off from the conservatives who had nominated him and helped elect him, preferring the counsel of big-government Democrats like former Texas Governor John Connally, Harvard professor Daniel Patrick Moynihan, and practitioners of *realpolitik* like Henry Kissinger.

Even so, conservatives were stunned when, in 1971, Nixon instituted and maintained for nearly three years wage and price controls of varying severity. Mounting disappointment with the administration erupted into anger when President Nixon announced that he was going to Peking. Support of the Republic of China on Taiwan and opposition to the People's Republic of China had been an article of faith with the Right since Mao Zedong seized control of the mainland in 1949. In the August 10, 1971, issue of *National Review*, 12 prominent conservatives, led by William F. Buckley, Jr., announced they were suspending "support of the administration."[30] The dozen signers were in effect the executive committee of the American conservative movement, and their joint declaration could not be ignored, certainly not by a president who was running behind his principal Democratic opponent (Senator Edmund Muskie of Maine) in the polls.

The president privately pledged that in return for the conservatives' support, Agnew would again be his running mate in 1972; the proposed Family Assistance Plan (a guaranteed annual income program for the poor) would be abandoned; and the defense budget would be increased modestly. The offer was too little, too late, and too obviously a political bribe. The "Manhattan Twelve" endorsed the idea of running a conservative against the president in the Republican primaries.

The only sitting officeholder who would take on Nixon was Congressman John Ashbrook of Ohio, chairman of the American Conservative Union, an architect of the Draft Goldwater movement, and one of the most principled conservatives in Washington. Ashbrook had always been a faithful Republican, but in his own words, he was "an American first, a conservative second, and a Republican third." He insisted that conservatives should stick firmly by their principles under both openly liberal administrations and nominally conservative administrations. Otherwise, the political agenda would "continue to be defined by the Left."[31]

In the eyes of most liberals, the Ashbrook challenge was "particularly feeble" and a "fizzle"[32]—the Ohio congressman received barely 10 percent of the vote in three primaries. But in the short term, the Ashbrook candidacy helped keep Agnew on the ticket (Nixon thought seriously about running with John Connally) and forced Nixon to address the explosive issue of busing in the Florida primary. In the long term, the Ashbrook campaign "preserved

Principled Politicians

Whittaker Chambers

(Born April 1, 1901; died July 9, 1961)

A former member of the American Communist Party, Chambers was the star
witness in the famous "Trial of the Century," the Hiss–Chambers trials, that sent
former State Department official Alger Hiss to jail. Reflecting on his experience,
this gifted writer and heroic witness to the truth wrote *Witness*—in which he
argued that the crisis of the twentieth century was a crisis of faith requiring man
to choose: God or Man, Soul or Mind, Freedom or Communism. He posthu-
mously received the Presidential Medal of Freedom in 1984.

CAREER
Writer for several Communist Party publications
Writer/Senior Editor, *Time Magazine*, 1939–1948
Senior Editor, *National Review*, late 1950s

SELECTED WRITINGS
Witness, 1952
Cold Friday, 1964
Odyssey of A Friend: Whittaker Chambers' Letters to William F. Buckley, Jr.,
    1954-1961, William F. Buckley, Jr., (ed.), 1970.
Ghosts on the Roof: Selected Journalism of Whittaker Chambers 1931–1959,
    Terry Teachout (ed.), 1989.

RECOMMENDED BIOGRAPHY
Whittaker Chambers: A Biography, Sam Tanenhaus, Random House, 1997

NOTABLE QUOTE
"The Communist vision is the vision of Man without God."
    —*Witness*, 1980

THE DIFFERENCE HE MADE
"For me, and others who knew him, his voice had been and still is like Kirsten
Flagstad's [Wagnerian soprano], magnificent in tone, speaking to our time from
the center of sorrow, from the center of the earth."
    —William F. Buckley, Jr., *National Review*, August 6, 2001
"When some future Plutarch writes his American Lives, he will find in Chambers

61

penetrating and terrible insights into America in the early twentieth century."

—Historian Arthur Schlesinger, Jr., quoted in *Witness*

"Chambers' three essential themes—the sense of titanic struggle, the interpretation of that struggle as God versus Man, and the belief in the fundamental continuity of liberalism and Communism—struck deep chords and became part of the conservative 'case' in the 1950s and beyond."

—Historian George H. Nash, *The Conservative Intellectual Movement in America Since 1945*

the conscience of the conservative movement" and demonstrated that conservatives within the Republican Party could not be taken for granted.[33] Goldwater started a conservative counterrevolution with his stubborn, splendid candidacy. Ashbrook kept the counterrevolution alive—with few workers and little money—when many conservatives were content to go along with the president.

According to Nixon aide H. R. Haldeman, Nixon talked frequently in 1972 about building a "new" party—an "Independent Conservative Party"—based on a coalition of Southern Democrats and conservative Republicans. The stated aim was to "get control of Congress without an election ... and make a truly historic change in the entire American political structure."[34] But any such realignment (daunting even after Nixon crushed liberal Democrat George McGovern in November, winning 49 states and almost 61 percent of the popular vote) faded as Watergate transmogrified from a third-rate burglary into a front-page scandal.

As conservatives expressed their disquiet about what one called a "squalid, disgraceful and inexcusable affair," Vice President Agnew—a favorite of conservatives for his blistering anti-liberal rhetoric—stunned the nation by resigning his office after pleading no contest to a charge of income tax evasion.[35] Agnew's plea was part of an agreement with prosecutors who were about to indict him on bribery charges. It was a measure of the new resilience of the conservative movement that Agnew's forced exit from national politics invoked sorrow and regret rather than dismay or panic. Conservatives should not make the mistake, said Bill Buckley, of defending Agnew as liberals had defended Alger Hiss. Rather, they should separate the "valid ideas" that Agnew espoused from the man himself.[36]

Throughout the rest of 1973 and into the spring and summer of 1974, Nixon sank deeper and deeper into the mire of Watergate. In March, Senator James Buckley of New York, brother of William, stated that Nixon should resign to preserve the presidency, but conservatives were reluctant to join the junior senator, at least publicly. Privately their dismay escalated, fueled by the ever-mounting evidence that Nixon was far more involved than he had allowed them to believe. In late July, the House Judiciary Committee approved three articles of impeachment, and any remaining possibility that Nixon might evade impeachment disappeared with the release on August 4, 1974, of his "smoking gun" conversations with Haldeman. The president had deliberately participated in an unconstitutional cover-up of Watergate.

When Nixon still clung to the mast of the White House and expressed the hope that the Senate would vote to acquit him, Senate Republicans met and decided that someone had to tell Nixon it was time for him to resign. They picked the man who had never hesitated to do what he thought was right for his party and his country—Barry Goldwater. "Mr. Conservative" never forgave Nixon for lying to him and the nation about his role in the Watergate affair and for failing to apologize publicly for turning a political scandal into a national tragedy.

NEW RIGHT AND OLD LEFT

During this chaotic period two new and influential branches of conservatism came into being. The New Right was a reaction to the attempted liberal takeover of the Republican Party—epitomized after Nixon's resignation in August 1974 by President Gerald Ford's selection of ultraliberal Nelson Rockefeller as his vice president. The neoconservatives similarly responded to the liberal seizure of the Democratic Party, represented by the nomination of George McGovern and the succeeding New Politics.

Political analyst Kevin Phillips was the first to use the label "New Right" when describing the collective efforts of Richard Viguerie, Paul Weyrich, Howard Phillips (no relation), and John (Terry) Dolan. They were true believers, firmly conservative and fiercely anti-communist, middle-class and middle American. They saw as their enemy the four "bigs" of modern America—Big Government, Big Business, Big Labor, and Big Media.

Viguerie was rightfully called the Godfather of the New Right because he raised most of its money, but the chief strategist was Paul Weyrich, a one-time newspaper reporter and radio–television journalist turned Washington political operative. With funding from Colorado businessman Joseph Coors and direct-mail assistance from Richard Viguerie, Weyrich founded or co-founded such key conservative institutions as The Heritage Foundation (started with a handsome $250,000 gift from Coors), the Committee for the Survival of a Free Congress, the American Legislative Exchange Council, and the Moral Majority, a major player in the political wars of the late 1970s and early 1980s. The New Right regarded itself as independent of the Republican Party and representative of all elements of conservatism. "I think," said Howard Phillips, "both the New Right—the iron fist—and the Old Right—the velvet glove—are necessary."[37]

At about the same time, a series of cataclysmic events jolted a small but influential group of old-fashioned liberals and forced them to move out of their no-longer-comfortable Democratic digs. These happenings included the presidential candidacy of George McGovern; the seeming willingness of modern liberals to let Vietnam and any other nation under siege fall into the hands of the communists; the refusal of prominent Democrats to fault the United Nations for its virulent anti-Israel rhetoric; and the revolution in sexual and social relations that produced what liberal critic Lionel Trilling called the "adversary culture."

"Mugged by reality" (one-time radical Irving Kristol's phrase), the neoconservatives attacked the radicals as despoilers of the liberal tradition. Kristol called for a return to the "republican virtue" of the Founding Fathers and invoked the idea of a good society. He endorsed the notion of a "moral and political order" and conceded that the idea of a "hidden hand" had its uses in the marketplace.[38] Conservatives welcomed Kristol warmly, with Buckley saying that he was "writing more sense in the public interest these days than anybody I can think of."[39]

The neoconservatives were not simply a small group of New York-based thinkers and writers. They were, as Theodore H. White put it, "action intellectuals" with connections to America's leading universities and the more important mass media, direct access to officeholders and the political elite, good relations with major elements of organized labor, and strong roots in influential foundations and think tanks with multi-million-dollar budgets.[40] They were uniquely qualified to carry the conservative message where no conservative had gone before.

Kristol and colleagues like Norman Podhoretz and Nathan Glazer helped to spawn as many neoconservative institutions as Richard Viguerie and Paul Weyrich did on the New Right. These included influential journals like *The Public Interest, The National Interest,* and *The New Criterion,* and organizations like the Coalition for a Democratic Majority (founded in the wake of McGovern's capturing of the presidential nomination) and the foreign-policy-oriented Committee on the Present Danger. And just as Weyrich forged a close relationship with benefactor Joseph Coors, Kristol found a generous supporter in William E. Simon, former secretary of the Treasury and president of the John M. Olin Foundation. The foundation put up $600,000 to start *The National Interest* and $100,000 to fund *The New Criterion.*

The New Right and the neoconservatives were not a natural alliance. The New Right was deeply suspicious of government, while the neoconservatives embraced it. The New Right loved the mechanics of politics, while the neoconservatives preferred the higher plane of public policy. But both hated communism and despised liberals—the New Right for what they had always been, the neoconservatives for what they had become. In the end, it was the neoconservatives' anti-communism and resistance to the counterculture that won the approval of the conservatives and led to a pragmatic marriage. The minister who presided over the nuptials was Ronald Reagan, who needed the brainpower of the neoconservatives and the manpower of the New Right, especially the Christian Right, to be elected.

Despite the urging of conservatives, new and old, Reagan hesitated to challenge incumbent Republican President Ford in 1976 for the presidential nomination. A turning point for the former California governor was Ford's refusal to meet with famed Russian dissident and author Alexander Solzhenitsyn. Reagan was placed on the defensive early on in the campaign by his controversial proposal to transfer a number of federal programs to the states without seeming to provide for their funding, as well as by a decision of campaign manager John Sears to mute the candidate's conservatism. Although a heavy favorite, Reagan narrowly lost the New Hampshire primary in March 1976 and then four more primaries in a row. Contributions dried up and conservative spirits sagged across the country. Almost everyone in the Reagan campaign was ready to concede; Nancy Reagan was convinced her husband would "embarrass" himself if he kept campaigning and losing.[41]

But the most important person of all was dead set against giving up. Reagan abandoned a "nice guy" strategy and, stung by Ford's personal attacks on him as extremist and misinformed, went after the president hard. He focused on gut issues like the Panama Canal, détente, and deficit spending. With the guidance of Senator Jesse Helms and the help of his formidable organization, Reagan campaigned 12 full days in North Carolina and won. M. Stanton Evans has described the contest in the Tarheel State as "the second most important primary in modern conservative politics," the first being the epic Goldwater–Rockefeller primary in California 12 years earlier.[42] If Reagan had failed in North Carolina, it is probable that he would have conceded to Ford and headed home to California and political irrelevance.

Instead, an exuberant Reagan went on to win a string of primaries, including those in Texas and California, but could not overcome the many advantages of presidential incumbency that Gerald Ford enjoyed. The convention ballot was heartbreakingly close: Ford, 1,187; Reagan, 1,070. The following day Reagan thanked his campaign advisers and workers, many of whom were weeping, and reminded them that although "we lost...the cause goes on." And then, tellingly, he added a couple of lines from an old Scottish ballad, "I'll lay me down and bleed awhile; though I am wounded, I am not slain. I shall rise and fight again."[43]

1 Remarks by Barry Goldwater, Young Republican rally, Dodger Stadium, Los Angeles, September 16, 1963, Human Events Library, Washington, D.C.

2 *Time*, October 3, 1963, pp. 34–35.

3 Theodore White, *The Making of the President—1964* (New York: Atheneum Publishers, 1965), pp. 135–137.

4 William Scranton to Barry Goldwater, July 12, 1964, in Scranton Papers, Pattee Library, Pennsylvania State University.

5 Barry M. Goldwater with Jack Casserly, *Goldwater* (New York: Doubleday, 1988), pp. 185–186.

6 Acceptance Address of Honorable Barry Goldwater, *Official Proceedings of the Twenty-Eighth Republican Convention*, Washington, D.C., 1964, p. 415.

7 *Ibid.*, pp. 418–419:

8 White, *The Making of the President—1964*, p. 228.

9 Anthony Lewis, "The Issues: Civil Rights, Extremism and Nuclear Policy Are the Major Themes Now," *The New York Times*, August 30, 1964.

10 Kathleen Hall Jamieson, *Packaging the Presidency: A History and Criticism of Presidential Campaign Advertising* (New York: Oxford University Press, 1992), p. 186.

11 *Ibid.*, pp. 198–199.

12 Warren Boroson, "What Psychiatrists Say About Goldwater," *Fact*, September–October 1964, pp. 24, 63.

13 Edwin Diamond and Stephen Bates, *The Spot: The Rise of Political Advertising on Television* (Cambridge, Mass.: MIT Press), 1988, p. 137.

14 *U.S. News & World Report*, December 21, 1964, p. 47.

15 Judis, *William F. Buckley Jr.*, pp. 230–231.

16 *Ibid.*, p. 232.

17 Reagan, *An American Life*, pp. 140–141.

18 Ronald Reagan, "A Time for Choosing," *Human Events*, November 28, 1964, pp. 8–9.

19 Stephen Hess and David Broder, *The Republican Establishment: The Present and the Future of the G.O.P.* (New York: Harper & Row), p. 253.

20 *Ibid.*, pp. 253–254; author's interview with Henry Salvatori, December 21, 1991.

21 Walter Lippmann, *Washington Post*, November 5, 1964; see James Reston in *The Road to the White House* (New York: *The New York Times*, 1965), p. 273.

22 William Knowland, quoted in Robert J. Donovan, *The Future of the Republican Party* (New York: New American Library, 1964; Ronald Reagan, *National Review*, November 17, 1964, p. 1001; Frank Meyer, *National Review*, December 1, 1964, p. 1057; "From the Phoenix Ashes," *Human Events*, November 14, 1964, p. 4.

23 See M. Stanton Evans, *The Future of Conservatism* (New York: Holt, Rineheart & Winston, 1968), p. 135.

24 Viguerie, *The New Right*, p. 27.

25 White, *The Making of the President—1964*, p. 409.

26 Author's interview with John Sears, June 9, 1992.

27 Robert Alan Goldberg, *Barry Goldwater*, p. 237.

28 William Rusher, *The Rise of the Right*, p. 212.

29 Richard M. Nixon to the author, November 4, 1992.

30 "A Declaration," *National Review*, August 10, 1971, p. 842.

31 Jack Rosenthal, "Ashbrook, Nixon's Rival on the Right, Finding Florida Campaign Trail Rough," *The New York Times*, February 15, 1972, and Charles Moser, *Promise and Hope*, (Washington, D.C., Free Congress Foundation, 1974), p. 8.

32 Don Oberdorfer, "Has Nixon Muzzled the Right?" *Arizona Republic*, June 21, 1972.

33 Moser, *Promise and Hope*, p. 36.

34 H. R. Haldeman, *The Haldeman Diaries: Inside the Nixon White House* (New York: Putnam, 1994), p. 444.

35 "Watergate or Waterloo?" *The Right Report*, April 1973, p. 1.

36 Goldwater, *With No Apologies*, p. 264.

37 Viguerie, *The New Right*, p. 63.

38 Nash, *The Conservative Intellectual Movement in America Since 1945*, pp. 314–315.

39 *Ibid.*

40 White, "The Action Intellectuals," p. 35.

41 Lyn Nofziger, *Nofziger* (Washington, D.C.: Regnery Publishing, Inc., 1992), p. 179.

42 Author's interview with M. Stanton Evans, May 10, 1996.

43 Frank van der Linden, *The Real Reagan* (New York: William Morrow and Company, 1981), p. 144.

Chapter 4

Governing Conservative

WINNING CONSERVATIVE

Far from considering him too old or too conservative, many Americans wanted Ronald Reagan to run again. The enthusiasm was fueled by the inept presidency of Jimmy Carter, who, confronted with double-digit inflation and interest rates, blamed the public, and who, when the Soviets invaded Afghanistan in December 1979, expressed amazement at such blatant disregard for the human rights of Afghans. A Harris poll revealed that the majority of voters liked Reagan's right-of-center philosophy while nearly 60 percent felt that he would "inspire confidence as President."[1] After all, he had proven himself, in the words of the *Los Angeles Times*, to be "an accomplished practitioner in the art of government" during his eight successful years as California's governor.[2]

In his formal announcement in November 1979, Reagan pledged a 30 percent tax cut; an orderly transfer of federal programs to the state and local levels (no billion-dollar gaffe this time); a revitalized energy program based on increased production of oil, natural gas, and coal; a long-range diplomatic and military strategy to meet the challenge of the Soviet Union; and a North American economic accord among the United States, Canada, and Mexico. He concluded with words that resonated with a people wondering whether their best days were behind them:

A troubled and afflicted mankind looks to us, pleading for

us to keep our rendezvous with destiny; that we will uphold the principles of self-reliance, self-discipline, morality and—above all—responsible liberty for every individual; that we will become that shining city on a hill.[3]

The 69-year-old conservative bested six of the GOP's brightest and best in the primaries: Senate Republican leader Howard Baker; former Treasury Secretary John Connally; Senator Bob Dole, the 1976 vice presidential nominee; Congressman Phil Crane, chairman of the American Conservative Union; liberal Congressman John Anderson, and George H. W. Bush, former everything, including U.S. envoy to China and chairman of the Republican National Committee. Bush provided the most formidable opposition, but after Reagan beat him in Texas, New York, and Oregon, Bush conceded the nomination.

The Republican National Convention in Detroit should have been all about the coming to power of conservatism with the adoption of a platform written by Senator Jesse Helms and Congressman Jack Kemp and the selection of Ronald Reagan as the party's presidential nominee. But former President Gerald Ford gave an unexpectedly dynamic speech on the opening night, and for two days there was intense excitement about the possibility of a "dream ticket" of Reagan and Ford. Then, after several meetings and talks, both men decided that neither the Constitution nor practical politics allowed for a co-presidency. Reagan turned to George Bush, who assured his one-time opponent that he could campaign "enthusiastically" for the platform and Reagan's election.[4]

Behind Reagan's nomination and ready to help him as he began his presidential campaign were dozens of conservative organizations involving thousands of people and spending millions of dollars annually—a counter-establishment only dreamed of by the most optimistic conservatives a decade before. They included the American

Conservative Union, sponsor of the annual Conservative Political Action Conference (CPAC); the ACU Education and Research Institute, which under M. Stanton Evans would create the National Journalism Center; the National Taxpayers Union and the National Tax Limitation Committee; the Pacific Legal Foundation and the Washington Legal Foundation. Think tanks like The Heritage Foundation and the Cato Institute helped to place conservative ideas at the center of the public policy debate. *The American Spectator* and *Conservative Digest* joined the ranks of conservative journals whose combined circulation topped half a million.

From the first day of campaigning, President Jimmy Carter depended upon the usual anti-conservative arsenal of charges, attempting to portray Reagan as a right-wing extremist opposed to peace, arms control, and working people. Reagan refused to be thrown off-course and went on courting the blue-collar, ethnic Catholic vote, concentrating on Carter's sorry economic record (double-digit inflation coupled with zero economic growth), and reassuring voters that he could handle the weighty duties of the presidency. He agreed to debate Carter one week before Election Day. During the debate, the president was tight-lipped and stood rigidly at his podium, rarely looking at this opponent. Reagan was calm, cool, and presidential. When Carter tried to link Reagan with the idea of making Social Security voluntary and argued that he had opposed Medicare, Reagan shook his head ruefully and said, "There you go again."[5] The Carter campaign of fear and misrepresentation collapsed in an instant.

Although most of the national polls said it would be a close election, Reagan won by an electoral landslide and more than 8 million votes. His political coattails were long and wide, helping the GOP to pick up 12 seats in the Senate, giving it majority control for the first time in a quarter of a century. Almost every observer concluded that the results constituted a broad mandate for Reagan to change the direction of American politics. *Newsweek* called Reagan's plan to cut spending *and* income taxes a "second New Deal potentially as profound in its impact as the first was a half century ago."[6]

GOVERNING CONSERVATIVE

President Reagan could count on something that would not have been available to Robert A. Taft or Barry Goldwater if they had been elected—the resources of a national conservative movement. Reagan could turn for ideas to think tanks like The Heritage Foundation, which responded with the 1,093-page *Mandate for Leadership* containing 2,000 specific recommendations to move the federal government in a conservative direction. The president himself passed out copies of the Heritage tome at the very first meeting of his Cabinet. He could call on groups like the American Conservative Union, the Committee for the Survival of a Free Congress, and the National Rifle Association for political muscle. He could staff his White House with professionals who had gotten their start in the movement, such as Edwin Meese III, Richard V. Allen, Martin Anderson, Anthony Dolan, and T. Kenneth Cribb, Jr. He could depend on the support of influential popularizers like George Will, Patrick J. Buchanan, and William F. Buckley, Jr. He could rely for guidance on the analytical skills of the editors and writers of a wide range of journals like *National Review, Human Events, The American Spectator, Commentary, Policy Review,* and the editorial pages of *The Wall Street Journal.*

Since his Hollywood days when he had turned over 91 percent of his earnings to the federal government, Reagan had been a devout believer in low taxes. He argued that if you reduced tax rates and allowed people to spend or save more of what they earned, "they'll be more industrious, they'll have more incentive to work hard, and money they earn will add fuel to the great economic machine that energizes our national progress." Some economists called this approach supply-side economics—"I call it common sense," said Reagan.[7]

It would take fireside chats with the American people, deals with "boll weevil" Democrats in the House of Representatives, pep talks with fatigued aides, and recovery from an attempted assassination, but on August 17, 1981, President Reagan signed the Economic Recovery Tax Act (ERTA) into law. The measure cut all income taxes by 25 percent, reduced the top marginal tax rate from 70 percent to 50 percent, and indexed tax rates to offset the impact of inflation. It took over a year for the recovery to kick in, but beginning in late 1982, the economy began 92 straight months of growth, the longest uninterrupted period of peacetime expansion since the government began keeping such statistics in 1854. Nearly 17 million new jobs were created by the time Reagan left office. Just under $20 trillion worth of goods and services, measured in actual dollars, was produced from 1982 to 1987.

There is no denying, however, that American indebtedness increased significantly during the Reagan years. The administration borrowed $1 for every $5 it spent, increasing the national debt by $1.5 trillion through 1988. But as a share of gross domestic product, the federal deficit fell sharply from 6 percent in 1985 to 3 percent in 1989. At the same time, the Reagan administration reduced inflation, lowered unemployment, cut the prime interest rate in half, and produced economic growth of 6 percent by 1983. If one examines the economic report cards of American presidents from Truman through Reagan, said Harvard economist Robert Barro, Reagan finishes first. In fact, summed up economist Richard B. McKenzie, the 1980s were, up to then, "the most prosperous decade in American history."[8]

A sizeable percentage of the increased spending was allotted to the U.S. military as part of Reagan's overall decision to defeat communism, not merely contain it. From intelligence reports and the insights accumulated over a lifetime of study and reading, the president concluded that communism was cracking and ready to crumble. Indeed, in one of the most memorable utterances of his presidency, Reagan predicted in 1982 (before the British Parliament at Westminster), "The march of freedom and democracy...will leave Marxism–Leninism on the ash-heap of history as it has left other tyrannies which stifle the freedom and muzzle the self-expression of the people."[9]

The administration pursued a multifaceted foreign policy offensive that included covert and other support to the Solidarity movement in Poland, a psychological operation to engender indecision and fear among Soviet leaders along with an increase in pro-freedom public diplomacy; a global campaign to reduce Soviet access to Western high technology; and a drive to hurt the Soviet economy by driving down the price of oil and limiting natural gas exports to the West. Another part of what came to be called the Reagan Doctrine was assistance to anti-communist forces in Afghanistan, Nicaragua, Angola, and Cambodia. The doctrine was among the most cost-effective of Cold War doctrines, costing the United States only about half a billion dollars a year and yet forcing the cash-strapped Soviets to spend 16 times that amount to deflect its impact. The success of the doctrine is unquestioned: It resulted in a Soviet pullout from Afghanistan, the election in 1990 of a democratic government in Nicaragua, and the removal of 40,000 Cuban troops from Angola.

For President Reagan, 1983 was a pivotal year. In March, he announced that development and deployment of a comprehensive anti-ballistic missile system would be his top defense priority. He called the system the Strategic Defense Initiative. The only people who hated it more than its liberal detractors in this country (who ridiculed it as "Star Wars") were the Soviets. A decade later, General Makhmut Gareer, who headed the department of strategic analysis in the Soviet Ministry of Defense, revealed what he had told the Soviet general staff and the Politburo in 1983: "Not only could we not defeat SDI, SDI defeated all our possible counter-measures."[10]

That same month, President Reagan stated that the West should recognize that the Soviets "are the focus of evil in this modern world" and the masters "of an evil empire."[11] Reagan was echoing the moral convictions of anti-communists who had preceded him, such as Robert Taft, Whittaker Chambers, Bill Buckley, and Barry Goldwater. Many conservatives consider Reagan's "evil empire" speech the most important of his presidency, a compelling example of what Czech President Vaclav Havel calls "the power of words to change history." When Reagan visited Poland and East Berlin after the collapse of Soviet communism, former dissidents told him that when he called the Soviet Union an "evil empire," it gave them enormous hope. Finally, they said to each other, America had a leader who "understood the nature of communism."[12]

Biographer Lou Cannon concluded that "no president save FDR defined a decade as strikingly as Ronald Reagan defined the 1980s."[13] In fact, Reagan left an indelible mark on American politics starting in the mid-1960s, when he was governor of California (where he instituted a welfare reform program that anticipated the federal welfare reform of the mid-1990s), blossoming through the eight years of his presidency, and continuing to this day. Even as the first half of the twentieth century has been called the Age of Roosevelt, the last half of the twentieth century can rightly be labeled the Age of Reagan.

Just as Franklin D. Roosevelt led America out of a great economic depression, Ronald Reagan lifted a traumatized country out of a
great psychological depression induced by the assassinations of John
F. Kennedy and Martin Luther King, Jr., and sustained by the Vietnam War, Watergate, and the Carter malaise. He used the same political instruments as Roosevelt—the major address to Congress and
the fireside chat with the people—and the same optimistic, uplift-
ing rhetoric. But although both Roosevelt and Reagan appealed to
the best in America, there was a significant philosophical difference
between the two presidents—Roosevelt turned first to government
to solve problems while Reagan turned first to the people.

George H. W. Bush was easily elected in the fall of 1988 (achiev-
ing a 426 to 112 triumph in the Electoral College over Democrat
Michael Dukakis) because he gave the electorate one more opportunity to vote for Reagan. Most conservatives accepted Bush as a
born-again conservative, noting his pledge of "no new taxes" and
his pro-life and strong law-and-order stance during the campaign.
They looked forward with anticipation to the Bush years and back-
ward with fondness and appreciation on the Reagan years.

The conservative movement had generally flourished during the
1980s: *National Review* and *The American Spectator* reached new circulation highs of 200,000 and over; *Human Events* topped 125,000. The
American Conservative Union drew as many as 1,000 activists to its
annual Conservative Political Action Conferences; and new organizations like the Family Research Council and the Competitive Enterprise Institute gathered strength. The Heritage Foundation doubled
its annual budget to nearly $18 million, and the Cato Institute
moved to Washington, D.C., and into an eight-story glass-walled
headquarters. Conservative think tanks sprang up in a dozen states.
Writers like Charles Murray, Michael Novak, Dinesh D'Souza,
George Gilder, and Marvin Olasky published influential and best-

selling books such as *Losing Ground* (Murray), *The Spirit of Democratic Capitalism* (Novak), *Illiberal Education* (D'Souza), *Wealth and Poverty* (Gilder), and *The Tragedy of American Compassion* (Olasky). Foundations like the Lynde and Harry Bradley Foundation, the John M. Olin Foundation, the Smith–Richardson Foundation, the Sarah Scaife Foundation, and the redoubtable Earhart Foundation disbursed in the aggregate millions of dollars each year to think tanks, academics, authors, and publications.

There were inevitable tensions within the movement as it grew in size and influence. In the 1950s the sharpest debates had been between traditionalists and libertarians as to the right balance between liberty and order. In the 1980s, traditionalists and neoconservatives disputed with each other over the proper role of the state, as at a 1986 Philadelphia Society meeting when conservative professor Stephen Tonsor deplored the "arrogance" of former Marxists and radicals dictating policies and beliefs to those who had never strayed from the truth. *American Spectator* editor R. Emmett Tyrrell, an early and enthusiastic publisher of Irving Kristol, replied that such criticism did not take into account how much "neoconservatives were suffering for the [conservative] cause."[14] The external threat of communism and the calming presence of Ronald Reagan persuaded most conservatives to sublimate their differences for the greater good. But with the collapse of communism and the departure of Reagan, disagreements between the varying kinds of conservatism came to the surface with more intensity.

MR. SPEAKER

Hell hath no fury like a conservative betrayed. President Bush had campaigned and won as a no-new-taxes conservative but in the second year of his presidency, his lips were saying something else. Technocrats in the White House and liberal Democrats on Capitol

Russell Kirk

(Born October 19, 1918; died April 29, 1994)

Russell Kirk was a prolific author, essayist, lecturer, and critic. Educated at Michigan State University, Duke University, and St. Andrews University in Scotland, this "master of letters" is best known for *The Conservative Mind*, a history of Anglo–American thought which made conservatism intellectually respectable and gave the conservative movement its name. Russell was the recipient of numerous awards, including the Presidential Citizens Medal, conferred on him by President Reagan in 1989.

CAREER

Editor, *The University Bookman*, 1960–1994

Founder and editor, *Modern Age*, 1957–1959

Syndicated columnist, 1962–1975

President, The Wilbur Foundation, 1979–1994

Editor, *The Library of Conservative Thought*, 1988–1994

Guggenheim Fellow, 1954–1955

Senior Fellow, The American Council of Learned Societies, 1948

Constitutional Fellow, the National Endowment for the Humanities, 1985

Fulbright Lecturer, Scotland, 1987

Distinguished Fellow, The Heritage Foundation, 1978–1994

SELECTED WRITINGS

The Conservative Mind: From Burke to Eliot, 1953

The American Cause, 1957

Old House of Fear, 1962

The Surly Sullen Bell and Other Stories, 1965

A Creature of the Twilight, 1966

Eliot and His Age: T.S. Eliot's Moral Imagination in the Twentieth Century, 1971

The Roots of American Order, 1974

Lord of the Hollow Dark, 1980

The Politics of Prudence, 1993

Governing Conservative

RECOMMENDED AUTOBIOGRAPHY

The Sword of Imagination: Memoirs of a Half-Century of Literary Conflict,
William B. Eerdmans Publishing Company, 1995.

NOTABLE QUOTE

"In essence, the conservative person is simply one who finds the permanent
things more pleasing than Chaos and Old Night."

—*The Politics of Prudence,* Intercollegiate Studies Institute, 1993

THE DIFFERENCE HE MADE

"It is inconceivable to imagine an important, let alone hope for a dominant,
conservative movement in America, without [Kirk's] labor."

—William F. Buckley, Jr., ISI Testimonial Dinner for Kirk, December 1991

"Dr. Kirk has helped renew a generation's interest and knowledge of
[the]...'permanent things,' which are the underpinnings and the intellectual
infrastructure of the conservative revival in our nation."

—Ronald Reagan, quoted in *The Unbought Grace of Life*

"Almost single-handedly [Kirk] rooted the American conservative movement in
the rich loam of the Western Christian tradition—and lived to see it triumph
over its twentieth-century adversaries."

—Former National Review publisher William A. Rusher, quoted in
The Sword of Imagination

Hill pressured the president to do something about the stagnant
economy, growing by barely 2 percent, and the rising federal deficits,
estimated at some $160 billion in 1990. For them, the solution was
obvious—raise taxes. Rejecting conservative arguments that new
taxes would slow economic growth and could lead to a recession,
Bush made a deficit-cutting deal with the Democratic Congress that
included tax revenue increases. "If George Bush had pardoned Willie
Horton or burned Old Glory on the lawn of the White House,"
reacted The Heritage Foundation's Daniel Mitchell, "it would hardly have rivaled the flip-flop he has committed on taxes." Vice Presi-

dent Dan Quayle later conceded that Bush's broken promise haunted him "for the rest of his presidency."[15]

It even cast a pall over Bush's impressive leadership in the Persian Gulf War, which was most Americans' idea of a perfect war— short, nearly bloodless, victorious, and in prime time. President Bush authorized the start of Operation Desert Storm on January 15, 1991, after months of congressional debate that culminated in a goahead resolution. After five weeks of punishing air and missile strikes, General H. Norman Schwarzkopf launched a two-front ground attack. Just 100 hours after coalition forces attacked, Bush ordered a cease-fire. Despite many predictions of massive U.S. casualties, only 148 Americans were killed in action, Kuwait was a sovereign nation again, and oil reserves essential to the West were rendered safe.

It seemed that the ghost of the Vietnam War was finally laid to rest. President Bush enjoyed extraordinary public approval ratings of some 90 percent, but in less than 18 months, Bush's approval plummeted nearly 60 points. The central reason was smoldering public dissatisfaction with a dipping economy. Median household income in 1991 fell 3.5 percent. Only one million new jobs were created in the first three and a half years of the Bush presidency—the worst record of any administration since World War II. Unemployment hit 7.7 percent, the highest since the 1982–1983 recession.

Confronted by a superb campaigner in Arkansas Governor Bill Clinton, a united Democratic Party, and a well-financed third-party nominee—billionaire Ross Perot—-Bush went down to defeat in November 1992. He received only 37.4 percent of the popular vote, less than Barry Goldwater had in his humiliating 1964 loss to Lyndon Johnson. Telling evidence of the public's widespread discontent was the 19 million votes cast for Perot, whose 18.9 percent of the total vote was the highest for an independent presidential candidate since 1912 when Theodore Roosevelt ran on the Bull Moose ticket. Bush "inherited an impregnable fortress from Mr. Reagan," wrote *National Review* editor John O'Sullivan, "and set assiduously about undermining the ramparts. All that Mr. Clinton did was lean on it." Heritage President Edwin J. Feulner insisted that America, and the conservative movement, owed George Bush a "great debt of gratitude" for his lifetime of service to the country, for standing firm on judicial appointments like Supreme Court Justice Clarence Thomas, and for steering the Persian Gulf War so skillfully. But on the twin issues most important to the majority of Americans, taxes and spending, he had "stumbled badly." Bush proved, said Feulner, that "a 'leader' without a cause is a leader without a following."[16] A new conservative leader with a carefully crafted cause now emerged from the other end of Pennsylvania Avenue.

The Contract with America was the tip of a giant conservative iceberg that in November 1994 tore into the seemingly permanent Democratic majority in Congress and sank it faster than the *Titanic.* The iceberg had been gathering mass for nearly 50 years. Before there was a Contract with America, there were seminal works like Hayek's *The Road to Serfdom* and Kirk's *The Conservative Mind*; best-sellers like Milton Friedman's *Free To Choose* and William Bennett's *The Book of Virtues*; grassroots political organizations like the Committee of One Million (Against the Admission of Communist China to the United Nations) and the Christian Coalition; interest groups like the National Right to Work Committee and the National Right to Life Committee. There were creative fundraisers like Richard Viguerie and John von Kannon; generous, patient donors like Joseph Coors and William Simon; prescient anti-communists like Sidney Hook and Robert Conquest; powerful broadcasters like Fulton Lewis, Jr., and Rush Limbaugh; budget-slashing congressmen like H. R. Gross of Iowa; and penitent isolationists like Everett Dirksen of Illinois.

There were skilled political operatives like F. Clifton White and successful businessmen like Amway founders Rich DeVos and Jay Van Andel and publisher Thomas Phillips.

And there were the three political leaders—Robert Taft, Barry Goldwater, and Ronald Reagan—on whose shoulders Newt Gingrich and all the other revolutionary congressmen stood as they prepared to seize what had been a Democratic citadel for 40 years.

In a 1990 Heritage Foundation lecture to young conservatives, Gingrich outlined a new Republican vision while quoting Goldwater, Reagan, Buckley, and Irving Kristol. Rejecting the old vision of balancing the budget above all, the Georgia congressman offered four goals that, if realized, would create "a prosperous, free country offering hope and opportunity to all"—integrity in government; physical safety for all citizens; a growing economy; a replacement for the bureaucratic state in education, welfare, health, and the environment.[17] Working with pollsters like Frank Luntz, Gingrich, Dick Armey of Texas, and other congressmen, House conservatives developed a blueprint for the future that would, they estimated, appeal to the supporters of Ross Perot, a key voting bloc.

The formal signing of the Contract with America on the steps of the U.S. Capitol on September 27, 1994, was a calculated media event with fervent prayers, a solemn Pledge of Allegiance, a spirited marching band, fluttering American flags, and bright red, white, and blue bunting. Gingrich's words matched the crusading spirit of the occasion: "Today on these steps we offer this contract as a first step toward renewing American civilization."[18] House Republicans believed they had a political winner. Every poll confirmed it. The balanced budget amendment, the line-item veto, welfare reform, term limits, the $500 tax credit for children, and an enforceable death penalty for capital crimes had 80 percent support from the public. Even regulatory reform, litigation reform, and Social Security reform had 60 percent public backing.

On Election Day, Republicans gained 52 seats and assumed a majority in the House of Representatives for the first time since Eisenhower was president. *The New York Times* called the Republican triumph "a political upheaval of historic proportions."[19] After eight years as the minority in the Senate, Republicans recaptured the upper house 52–48. The Republican tide swept over the states as well. Republicans increased their number of governorships to 30 and reached near parity in state legislatures, gaining a total of 482 seats. The GOP controlled the governor's mansion in eight of the nine most populous states and in states representing more than 70 percent of the population.

"Conservatism's long march," wrote columnist George Will, "began thirty years ago with Barry Goldwater's capture of the Republican Party."[20] Will did not go back far enough. The transformation of the GOP from a minority to a majority party actually began in 1945 with the U.S. publication of F. A. Hayek's *The Road to Serfdom*, closely followed by the first major conservative victory of the postwar period—the election of the Republican 80th Congress and the emergence of Robert Taft as a national leader.

But the year that began with such shining promise ended in bitter disappointment. The Republican House watched its public approval sink from 52 percent in December 1994 to the upper 20s in January 1996, shortly after the two shutdowns of the federal government, which were blamed on the Republicans. Speaker Gingrich, the man of the hour in January, became the "Grinch who stole Christmas," with a perilous disapproval rating of 51 percent. Only five of the 21 legislative priorities in the Contract with America were enacted by Congress because of President Clinton's skillful opposi-

Robert Nisbet

(Born September 30, 1913; died September 9, 1996)

As the author of the classic *The Quest for Community* and other widely quoted works on man's relationship with man, Robert Nisbet became the most influential conservative sociologist in postwar America. Over the course of a career that spanned nearly 60 years, Nisbet served as dean of a new liberal arts college in California; taught at the University of California at Berkeley, the University of Arizona, and Columbia University; and was a resident scholar at the American Enterprise Institute.

CAREER

Instructor, Assistant Professor, Assistant Dean,
   University of California at Berkeley, 1939–1953
Brief stint in U.S. Military, 1944–1946
Dean, University of California at Riverside, 1953–1963
Visiting Professor, University of Bologna, 1956–1957
Professor, University of California at Riverside, 1963–1972
Professor, University of Arizona, 1972–1974
Albert Schweitzer Chair of Humanities, Columbia University, 1974–1978
Resident Scholar, The American Enterprise Institute, 1978–1980
Adjunct Scholar, The American Enterprise Institute, 1980–1986

SELECTED WRITINGS

The Quest for Community: A Study in the Ethics of Order and Freedom, 1953
Tradition and Revolt, 1968
The Degradation of Academic Dogma: The University in America, 1945-1970, 1971
The Social Philosophers, 1973
Twilight of Authority, 1975
The Social Philosophers, 1982
Prejudices: A Philosophical Dictionary, 1982
Conservatism: Dream and Reality, 1986
The Making of Modern Society, 1986
Roosevelt and Stalin: A Failed Courtship, 1988

The Present Age: Progress and Anarchy in Modern America, 1988

RECOMMENDED BIOGRAPHY

Robert Nisbet: Communitarian Traditionalist, Brad Lowell Stone, ISI Books, 2004

NOTABLE QUOTE

"The quest for community will not be denied for it springs from some of the powerful needs of human nature—needs for a clear sense of cultural purpose, membership, status, and continuity."

—*The Quest for Community*

THE DIFFERENCE HE MADE

"Nisbet is recognized by his admirers and detractors alike as one of the most original and influential American social theorists of his generation."

—Biographer Brad Lowell Stone, *Robert Nisbet: Communitarian Traditionalist*

"Nisbet was a man who always marched to his own drummer."

—Publisher Irving Louis Horowitz, quoted in *Robert Nisbet: Communitarian Traditionalist*

"[Reaganism is] the triumph of Nisbetism as the stated creed of American politics at the highest level."

—Author–editor Nicholas Lemann, *Washington Monthly,* September 1991

tion and use of the veto, and the Republicans' failure to respond forcefully to the Democrats' propaganda war.

Gingrich and his House colleagues mistakenly assumed that Clinton had no choice but to accept deep cuts in the budget to avoid shutting down the government. They recalled that President Reagan, not Congress, had been blamed by the media and the public for the last government shutdowns in the 1980s. But Clinton began vetoing and several congressional Republicans began revealing their lack of enthusiasm for truly changing the way Washington worked. "Republicans mistook public dissatisfaction with excesses in government," said one Democrat, "for hatred of government. People are not ready for a radical repudiation of a governmental role in society."[21]

The parallels between the Gingrich 104th Congress and the Taft 80th Congress are revealing. The Republican majorities in both were ruled by hubris, failing to make the critical distinction between winning a battle and winning a war. They sorely misjudged the political skills of the president they faced. They took the people for granted, neglecting to keep communicating what they were doing and why. Out of power for many years, they did not know how to govern consistently. The two Congresses also suffered from Caesarization—they rose and fell along with the reputations of their leaders. At the root of the problem for both the 80th Congress and the 104th Congress was the political reality that governing from Congress is almost impossible, particularly in the modern media age. Presidential power is too great and congressional power is too diffuse for Congress to prevail over the president for more than a limited time.

A REAGAN DEMOCRAT

Normally a presidential election is a referendum on the president's conduct of domestic and foreign policy. But 1996 offered a second national referendum—on the Republican "revolution" in government. By their votes, Americans would indicate their approval of the GOP's proposed downsizing and devolution of government. In the fall, Bob Dole ran an aggressive but unfocused campaign, failing, for example, to embrace the idea of an across-the-board tax cut of 15 percent until it was too late. He also neglected to work closely with many elements of the conservative coalition that had produced the Reagan and Bush victories of the 1980s. The social issues such as partial-birth abortion were never seriously addressed.

Bill Clinton was the first Democratic president since Franklin D. Roosevelt to win re-election and the first Democrat ever to be elected with an opposition Congress. He defeated Dole 49 percent to

41 percent, carrying 33 states with 379 electoral votes, including the golden prize of California. Ross Perot was again on the ticket, this time as the Reform Party candidate, but gained only 7.9 million votes, less than half his 1992 total. He won no electoral votes. The "sucking sound" heard was Perot's diminishing impact on American politics. Despite the most virulent anti-Congress rhetoric since 1948, Republicans retained control of the House, and increased their margin in the Senate.

In his 1997 State of the Union address, President Clinton positioned himself right of center, promising a balanced budget by 2002 and urging citizen volunteerism in a wide variety of fields. He offered a "new kind of government—not to solve all our problems for us, but to give all our people the tools to make the most of their own lives."[22] Conservatives accused Clinton of trying to imitate Reagan, which was true, but his attempted transformation confirmed that conservative ideas dominated the national political debate. The following year Clinton presented a glowing report of a nation prosperous and peaceful because of his policies but then tacked left by offering an expansive domestic agenda. The legislative agenda was soon eclipsed by the burgeoning scandal over the president's sexual relationship with a 21-year-old White House intern and the ensuing allegations of perjury and obstruction of justice.

In October the House of Representatives authorized an open-ended impeachment inquiry, and Speaker Gingrich made the fateful decision to use the Clinton scandal to galvanize Republican support in some 30 congressional races, mostly in the South. Ignoring the transparency of our media society, Gingrich and other Republicans believed they could run a series of local television ads attacking the president, at a cost of $25 million, without attracting national notice. Instead, the anti-Clinton commercials were seized upon by the Democrats to turn out their core constituencies, particularly Southern blacks. Republicans posted a net loss of five seats in the House and no gain in the Senate. Gingrich was immediately pilloried for failing to deliver the gain of 20 to 30 House seats he had predicted.

When a prominent conservative congressman declared he would challenge Gingrich for the speakership, Gingrich stepped down as Speaker and resigned his seat in the House as well. He decided that his party would be better served by his "voluntary" departure than by a bitter and divisive battle to retain power. His decision was influenced by a noticeable lack of support for him within the conservative movement. Where they had respected Taft, loved Goldwater, and idolized Reagan, conservatives by the fall of 1998 barely tolerated Gingrich as a result of his legislative compromises, especially his failure to challenge vigorously a $1.7 trillion federal budget. Following the disappointing 1998 election, not one major conservative leader, publication, or organization (with the exception of the Speaker's most loyal ally, Grover Norquist of Americans for Tax Reform) came forward to argue that Gingrich should remain as Speaker.

Nevertheless, Gingrich's place in political history is secure. The Contract with America was brilliant politics and led directly to the historic 1994 capture of the House. His leadership, with all its flaws, produced three straight Republican Houses in 1994, 1996, and 1998—the first such string of GOP victories in 70 years—and laid the foundation for the Republican congressional gains in 2000 and 2002. His reforms reshaped the House of Representatives, strengthening the Speaker's authority, reducing the power of the committee chairmen, and empowering backbenchers. He recruited dozens of candidates and raised millions of dollars, vitalizing the Republican Party and the conservative movement. He spawned conservative ideas, issues, and programs that are readily used by Members of Congress to this day. Historian Alvin S. Felzenberg sees parallels between Reagan and Gingrich in their courage, discipline, and commitment to a long march. It took Reagan 16 years—from 1964 to 1980—to win the presidency. It took Gingrich 16 years—from his first congressional victory in 1978 to the Contract with America in 1994—to win the House of Representatives. Each man, says Felzenberg, was "willing to be the only one to believe" he could succeed.[23]

1   Lee Edwards, *Ronald Reagan: A Political Biography* (Houston: Nordland Publishing, 1981), p. 188.

2   *Ibid.*

3   Lou Cannon, *President Reagan: The Role of a Lifetime* (New York: Simon and Schuster, 1991), p. 247.

4   "George Bush on His Role as No. 2," *U.S. News & World Report*, July 28, 1990, pp. 23–24.

5   Jeff Greenfield, *The Real Campaign* (New York: Summit Books, 1982), p. 241.

6   Lee Edwards, *Ronald Reagan*, p. 255.

7   Martin Anderson, *Revolution* (San Diego: Harcourt Brace Javonovich, 1988), p. 232.

8   Richard B. McKenzie, *What Went Right in the 1980s* (San Francisco: Pacific Research Institute, 1993), p. 1.

9   Ronald Reagan, *Speaking My Mind* (New York: Simon and Schuster, 1989), p. 118.

10 Daniel O. Graham, *Confessions of a Cold Warrior* (Fairfax, Va.: Preview Press, 1995), p. 153.

11 For Reagan's discussion of the phrase, see Reagan, *An American Life*, pp. 568–571.

12 Vaclav Havel, "Words on Words," *New York Review of Books*, January 18, 1990, p. 58, and Dinesh D'Souza, *Ronald Reagan: How an Ordinary Man Became an Extraordinary Leader* (New York: Free Press, 1997), p. 135.

13 Cannon, *President Reagan*, p. 831.

14 Paul Gottfried, *The Conservative Movement*, revised edition (New York: Twayne, 1993), pp. 91–92.

15 Daniel J. Mitchell, "Bush's Deplorable Flip-Flop on Taxes," Heritage Foundation *Executive Memorandum*, June 29, 1990; Dick Williams, *Newt! Leader of the Second American Revolution* (Marietta, Ga.: Longstreet Press, 1995), p. 127.

16 John O'Sullivan, "ITYS, Number 453," *National Review*, November 30, 1992, p. 6, and Edwin J. Feulner, Jr., "A New 'Mandate' for Limited Government," The Heritage Foundation, January 4, 1993.

17 Newt Gingrich, "The Washington Establishment vs. the American People," Heritage Foundation *Lecture* No. 279, August 22, 1990.

18 Judith Warner and Max Berley, *Newt Gingrich: Speaker to America* (New York: Penguin, 1995), pp. 182–183.

19 "Dr. Fell's Election," *The New York Times*, November 10, 1994.

20 George Will, "Reagan's Third Victory," *The Washington Post*, November 10, 1994.

21 *CQ Almanac*, 104th Congress, 1st Session, 1995, p. 11.

22 James Bennett, "President, Citing Education as Top Priority of 2nd Term, Asks for a 'Call to Action,'" *The New York Times*, February 5, 1997.

23 Author's interview with Alvin S. Felzenberg, January 1, 1998.

Chapter 5

The Role of the Movement

THE TWO PRESIDENCIES OF GEORGE W. BUSH

No U.S. president in his first year was as coolly welcomed and then warmly praised by the American public as George W. Bush. Bush's beginning was overshadowed by the disputed nature of his victory—narrowly losing the popular vote to Democrat Al Gore and winning the Electoral College by just one vote more than the needed 270. Widely described—and not only by partisan Democrats—as the man who "stole" the 2000 election, a cautious Bush began his presidency by focusing on taxes and education as a reflection of his "compassionate conservatism." Although the president seemed detached and even uncomfortable in the job, he was receiving modestly favorable public approval ratings of 57 percent (and much higher marks from conservatives) by mid-July. His major accomplishment was a monumental tax cut of $1.6 trillion, although most of the reductions were scheduled for later in the decade.

By early fall, there were signs—unemployment up, sales down, stagnant growth—that the country was close to, if not already in, a recession. But no politician wanted to be the first to use the "r" word. After all, America was the strongest, most prosperous nation in the world and probably in human history. If the occupant of the White House did not seem to be destined for greatness, what difference did it make? Then came September 11. The hijacked airplanes that smashed into the silver towers of the World Trade Center in New York City, the mammoth Pentagon in Washington, D.C., and the Pennsylvania countryside, killing nearly 3,000 innocent people, swept away the political and social detritus of the previous 10 months. The nation was no longer divided into red and blue (as depicted in a much-reproduced electoral map of the 2000 presidential results), but united in red, white and blue.

No more a remote chief executive, President Bush moved to rally Congress, our overseas allies, and the public. Congress overwhelmingly authorized an initial $40 billion for the war on terrorism. NATO invoked Article 5 of its charter for the first time ever, declaring that an attack on one member was an attack on all. And a tidal wave of patriotism inundated the nation. Aided by the public's tendency to rally around the president in a time of crisis as well as his decisive leadership, Bush's approval ratings skyrocketed until they topped 90 percent, the highest level of any president since the advent of polling. There were other reasons for the president's remarkable popularity. He turned out to be a good communicator, who, if not in the rhetorical league of Ronald Reagan or Bill Clinton, was able to bring Members of Congress repeatedly to their feet during an address to a joint session of Congress eight days after the terrorist attacks. And he delivered on his promise to oust quickly the radical Taliban government in Afghanistan and put terrorist leader Osama bin Laden on the run.

The president who had once retreated to the isolation of his Texas ranch whenever he could was now a constant and reassuring presidential presence, rarely out of sight. And the Jeffersonian Republican who favored limited, decentralized government now called for the authority to fight a protracted conflict, help industries hit hard by terrorism, and rejuvenate a stalled economy. Far from having a nervous breakdown over the first major terrorist attack on their soil—as some left-wing intellectuals had predicted—Americans remained as calm and as collected as their president. "The can-do pioneers who tamed a wild continent," wrote *The Economist*, "and then helped to win three world confrontations have not disappeared after all."[1]

By the first part of 2004, a presidential election year, Bush's popularity leveled off to the low 50s. Bipartisanship in Congress was virtually abandoned as the fundamental differences between Republicans and Democrats surfaced on core issues like taxes, spending, abortion, and gay marriage. Patriotism became passé in some quarters, especially in the academy. But America will not return to its pre–September 11 way of life. The terrorist attacks were a defining moment in modern American history, like the Japanese bombing of Pearl Harbor in December 1941.

In a time of crisis, according to the *New York Times*, a primary responsibility of the president is to "give Americans confidence in themselves and their ability to defeat the enemy."[2] George W. Bush has handled that responsibility, so far, as well as almost any other president in modern times. But the testing is far from over. Bush's leadership will be scrutinized as America and its allies consider what action to take next against terrorism. The president's success in liberating Iraq from the totalitarian grip of Saddam Hussein after barely one month of conflict and with minimal American casualties earned him high public approval. But serious questions have been raised about the failure so far to find conclusive evidence of weapons of mass destruction in Iraq—a primary argument for going to war with Saddam—as well as whether we are "occupiers" or "liberators" in post–Saddam Iraq.

The president's tax cuts have resulted in impressive economic growth, but the number of new jobs is lower than in the period following Reagan's tax cuts. And Bush has run up historic federal deficits. Now, confronted by a Democratic Party united behind a formidable candidate in Senator John Kerry of Massachusetts, President Bush must persuade the public in this election year that his policies regarding peace and prosperity are the right policies. He will be judged on his performance as CEO of the economy, commander in chief of the armed forces, and head of state. As in all campaigns, the president will utilize the five basic elements of politics—money, organization, his own skills as a campaigner, issues, and the media. In what promises to be another close election, Bush is fortunate in that he can call upon the myriad resources of a mature conservative movement to help him—a movement that has matured from a gaggle of brilliant but fractious individuals into a billion-dollar "Counter-Establishment of the Right," replete with its own training schools, think tanks (there are now some 40 state public policy research organizations), publications, foundations, book clubs, buildings, newspaper columnists (including Number One Cal Thomas), television and radio talk show hosts (led by Bill O'Reilly and Rush Limbaugh), film stars and producers (Mel Gibson is both), Nobel laureates, Pulitzer Prize winners, preachers and priests, entrepreneurs, novelists (Tom Wolfe is alive and well and writing), and political leaders from the White House to the city council.

How decisive or problematic the help will be depends upon the movement's philosophers, popularizers, philanthropists, and politicians. Will the thinkers, for example, continue to articulate a clearly defined consistent philosophy, based on the Declaration of Independence and the Constitution? Will the interpreters remain principled, or will they pander to the impulse of the moment to remain popular?

In the spring of 2003, *National Review* featured a cover article by David Frum (a former speechwriter for President George W. Bush), who declared war on paleoconservatives, calling them "unpatriotic" conservatives who should be read out of the movement for "turning their backs on their country" and failing to support the war on terrorism. Chairman David Keene of the American Conservative Union responded that Frum had painted "with far too broad a brush" and that while he supported the war in Iraq, he did not like "nation-building."[3] As the rhetoric from all sides escalated, veteran conservatives such as Donald Devine (who headed the Office of Personnel Management under President Reagan) called for a return to Frank Meyer's fusionist conservatism. That is, that conservatives should absorb the best of the various branches of the conservative mainstream and forge a consensus as the Founding Fathers did so brilliantly at the writing of the Constitution over two centuries ago.

However, the Iraqi war revealed sharp differences among conservatives about the proper conduct of American foreign policy in a post-communist world. Patrick Buchanan, representing the Old Right, vociferously opposed the war and U.S. "occupation" of Iraq in *The American Conservative*. William Kristol, invariably described as a neoconservative, as strongly supported the war and a policy of preemptive action against terrorism when necessary in *The Weekly Standard*. Editor Rich Lowry took a more nuanced position, sometimes praising President Bush, sometimes criticizing him, in the venerable *National Review*. As the sharp debate over the lessons of the Iraqi war and its aftermath continued, Owen Harries, the former editor of the neoconservative *National Interest*, quoted Edmund Burke—a favorite of traditional conservative Russell Kirk—on the potential danger of excessive governmental power.

"We may say that we shall not abuse this astonishing and hitherto unheard of power," Burke wrote of the Colossus-like British empire in the 1770s. "But every other nation will think we shall abuse it. It is impossible but that, sooner or later, this state of things must produce a combination against us which may end in our ruin."[4]

Because a viable movement requires a constant infusion of funds, it needs to be asked whether the number of conservative contributors—especially the golden donors—will grow or shrink? How many of the e-commerce millionaires and billionaires will support conservative ideas and institutions—what Edmund Burke called the "small platoons" of society? And will the politicians be able to translate successfully conservative principles into policies and programs that promote political and economic liberty at home and abroad?

Limited government, individual freedom and responsibility, the free market, a strong national defense, a belief in God—these are the core beliefs, bounded by the Constitution, on which American conservatism rests. Political leaders like Taft, Goldwater, Reagan, and Gingrich sought to govern by them. They did not always succeed, being human, but their failures occurred because they failed conservatism, not because conservatism failed them.

The transforming power of modern conservatism over the last 50 years has been unmistakable. In the late 1940s, we seemed to be headed for a socialist world in which despots like Stalin and Mao could only be contained, not defeated. In the 1990s, we celebrated the collapse of communism and the adoption of liberal democracy and free markets around the world because of the leadership of charismatic conservatives like Ronald Reagan and Margaret Thatcher.

The impacts of modern conservatism here at home have been equally profound. There is public distaste for ever-bigger government, a "leave us alone" attitude that stretches back as far as the Founding. Because of conservative initiatives, writes former Education Secretary William J. Bennett, several of the nation's leading cultural indicators, such as violent crime, the number of Americans on welfare, the teenage suicide rate, and the child poverty rate, have declined sharply, although the disturbing break-up of the family continues.[5] In the wake of September 11, 2001, a prudential internationalism has evolved, based on a simple principle—act multilaterally when possible and unilaterally when necessary.

The liberal historian Arthur Schlesinger, Jr., wrote in 1947 that "there seems no inherent obstacle to the gradual advance of socialism in the United States through a series of New Deals." Five-and-a-half decades later, the conservative columnist George Will wrote that we had experienced "the intellectual collapse of socialism."[6]

The one political constant throughout these five decades has been the rise of the Right, whose path to national power and prominence was often interrupted by the death of its leaders, calamitous defeats at the polls, constant feuding within its ranks over means and ends, and the perennial hostility of the prevailing liberal establishment. But through the power of its ideas—ever linked by the priceless principle of ordered liberty—and the unceasing dissemination and application of those ideas, the conservative movement has become a major and often the dominant player in the political and economic realms of the nation.

1 "America the Sensible," *The Economist*, October 27, 2001.

2 "A Homeland Pep Talk," *The New York Times*, November 9, 2001.

3 David Frum, "Unpatriotic Conservatives: A War Against America," *National Review*, April 7, 2003, p. 40, and David Keene, "Big Tent Needed for Conservatives of Every Stripe," *The Hill*, June 3, 2003.

4 Owen Harries, "What Conservative Means," *The American Conservative*, November 17, 2003.

5 William J. Bennett, *The Index of Leading Cultural Indicators 2001* (Washington, D.C.: The Heritage Foundation, 2001), pp. 2–3.

6 For the Schlesinger quote in *Partisan Review*, c. 1947, see "Notable and Quotable," *The Wall Street Journal*, December 27, 1961. For the Will quote, see Morton C. Blackwell, "Social Change and Friends of Liberty," an address delivered at the Mercatus Center, Arlington, Virginia, July 16, 2001.

BIBLIOGRAPHY

I have divided the following non-fiction books into four categories: a canon of eight works; 11 recommended books; two histories about modern conservatism; and four books that helped shape my particular brand of traditional conservatism.

THE CANON

The Road to Serfdom, Friedrich A. Hayek. A powerful polemic that argues, convincingly, that "planning leads to dictatorship" and that the direction of economic activity requires the "suppression of freedom." Published in 1944, it is the first defining work of the modern conservative movement.

Ideas Have Consequences, Richard A. Weaver. This tightly reasoned work asserts that ideas like nominalism, rationalism, and materialism have produced the moral "dissolution" of the West. Yet, says the author, mankind can recover from the scourge of modernism through a defense of private property, a respect for language, and an attitude of piety.

Witness, Whittaker Chambers. A dramatic, autobiographical story of communist spies, espionage, and betrayal that contains an apocalyptic warning about the epic battle being waged between the West and its totalitarian enemies. The most influential anti-communist book of the post–World War II era.

The Conservative Mind, Russell Kirk. A monumental history of Anglo–American conservative thinkers and politicians from the late 1700s through the middle of the twentieth century. With one book, Kirk established that a tradition of American conservatism had existed since the Founding of the Republic and made conservatism intellectually respectable.

The Quest for Community, Robert Nisbet. A classic study of how the community satisfies some of the most powerful needs of human nature—cultural purpose, membership status, and continuity. Echoing Alexis de Tocqueville and Edmund Burke, Nisbet calls for a rejuvenation of "intermediate associations" such as the family, the church, and the neighborhood.

God and Man at Yale, William F. Buckley, Jr. The first book by the renaissance man of the conservative movement documents how an anti-Christian, collectivist bias is corrupting his alma mater—and by implication American higher education.

Democracy in America, Alexis de Tocqueville. A brilliant sociological study by a nineteenth century French aristocrat and visitor to the United States who wrote that the maintenance of a democratic republic depends not only on the laws and institutions of a nation but on the manners and customs of its people.

The Federalist, Alexander Hamilton, James Madison, John Jay. An authoritative and profound explanation of the Constitution that is, in James Q. Wilson's words, "the single most important piece of American political philosophy ever written."

RECOMMENDED

What Is Conservatism? Frank Meyer. A far-ranging anthology of the leading conservative and libertarian thinkers of the day (circa 1964) attesting, editor Meyer argues, to the essential intellectual cohesiveness of the conservative movement.

Memoirs of a Superfluous Man, Albert Jay Nock. A superbly written and deeply pessimistic book about America's future that looks to a small Remnant of intellectuals to preach about the dangers of the ever-aggrandizing State.

Economics in One Lesson, Henry Hazlitt. A lucid analysis of the "dismal science" that outlines the intrinsic flaws of Keynes and Marx and the superiority of capitalism. Now dated, it is among the all-time best-selling conservative books.

The Theme Is Freedom: Religion, Politics and the American Tradition, M. Stanton Evans. A "modest counter-history" that demonstrates cogently how Western liberty and America's free institutions are the products of our religious faith and cannot survive without it.

Reflections of a Neoconservative: Looking Back, Looking Ahead, Irving Kristol. An authoritative, autobiographical look at the development of the neoconservative mind by the "godfather" of neoconservatism.

The Spirit of Democratic Capitalism, Michael Novak. A one-time socialist's clear-eyed inquiry into the "moral vision" of capitalism and the abject failure of socialism to work in practice anywhere.

A Humane Economy, Wilheim Roepke. This work, called the "very model of fusionism" by George A. Nash, combines an economist's defense of the free market with a conservative's defense of Christian humanism and a sharp criticism of "modern mass society."

Free to Choose, Milton Friedman. A compelling case for the essential connection between capitalism and freedom by the Nobel Prize-winning economist. It was the basis for a 10-part television series and became an international best seller.

Wealth and Poverty, George Gilder. A bold examination of the social, political, and economic forces that make up "supply-side economics"—the theory that dominated the domestic policies of the Reagan administration.

The Roots of American Order, Russell Kirk. The intellectual historian of the conservative movement lists them as the Hebrew understanding of the Covenant, Hellenic philosophy, Roman law and moral concepts, Christian doctrine, English common law and parliamentary government, and the American Founding.

The Black Book of Communism, Stephane Courtois and five others. Written by former-leftist French intellectuals, this is the best single volume about the crimes, terror, repression, and 100 million victims of communism in the twentieth century.

ABOUT CONSERVATISM

The Conservative Intellectual Movement in America Since 1945, George H. Nash. The definitive intellectual history of the modern conservative movement and a book about which it can be truly said, "Must reading for the inquiring conservative."

The Conservative Revolution: The Movement That Remade America,
Lee Edwards. The political equivalent of Nash's intellectual history, centered on Robert A. Taft, Barry Goldwater, Ronald Reagan, and Newt Gingrich, whom the author calls the "Four Misters" of American conservatism.

BOOKS THAT MADE A DIFFERENCE

Reclaiming the American Dream, Richard C. Cornuelle. A passionate, optimistic book about the potential power of the Independent Sector—the nation's vast network of non-government, non-commercial organizations which, if properly motivated, could solve many of America's economic and social problems.

The God That Failed, Richard Grossman, editor. Six famous ex-communists—Andre Gide, Richard Wright, Ignazio Silone, Stephen Spender, Arthur Koestler, and Louis Fischer—explain why they were initially attracted to communism and why they finally rejected it.

The Conscience of a Conservative, Barry Goldwater. One of the most influential political manifestos in American history, this 123-page book proclaimed a major new force in national politics—conservatism—and inspired countless young conservatives to enter the political world.

The Seven Storey Mountain, Thomas Merton. The spiritual document of a worldly, many-talented young man who became a Trappist monk—hailed by Fulton J. Sheen as "a 20th-century form of *The Confessions of St. Augustine.*"

ABOUT THE AUTHOR

Lee Edwards is Distinguished Fellow in Conservative Thought in the B. Kenneth Simon Center for American Studies at The Heritage Foundation.

A prolific writer, Dr. Edwards has been published in *Reader's Digest* and *National Review*, as well as leading newspapers, including the *Wall Street Journal, Los Angeles Times, Boston Globe, San Francisco Chronicle, Detroit News,* and *Washington Times.* His 15 books range from *Ronald Reagan: A Political Biography,* written in 1967, to *Educating for Liberty: The First Half Century of ISI,* written in 2003, and include *Missionary for Freedom: The Life and Times of Walter Judd; Goldwater: The Man Who Made a Revolution;* and *The Conservative Revolution: The Movement that Remade America.*

Educated at Duke University, the Sorbonne (Paris), and the Catholic University of America, Dr. Edwards was a fellow at the John F. Kennedy School of Government at Harvard University and is now an adjunct professor of politics at the Catholic University of America. He was founding director of the Institute on Political Journalism at Georgetown University, is the former president of The Philadelphia Society, and is currently chairman of the Victims of Communism Memorial Foundation.

Dr. Edwards and his wife, Anne, reside in Alexandria, Virginia.